World University Library

The World University Library is an interna   .al series
of books, each of which has been specially commissioned.
The authors are leading scientists and scholars from all over
the world who, in an age of increasing specialisation, see the
need for a broad, up-to-date presentation of their subject.
The aim is to provide authoritative introductory books for
students which will be of interest also to the general
reader. The series is published in Britain, France, Germany,
Holland, Italy, Spain, Sweden and the United States.

An illustration from Descartes' *Tractatus de Homine*.
The pineal gland is shown as the intermediary conveying
the physical sensation of warmth to the mind.

Raymond Greene

Human Hormones

World University Library

Weidenfeld and Nicolson
5 Winsley Street London W1

Photoset by BAS Printers Limited, Wallop, Hampshire
Manufactured by LIBREX, Italy

Contents

Part 2: Hormone effects on body functions

Preface

This book is intended for readers with some knowledge and interest in science but who have no special training in physiology or medicine. It has not proved easy to walk the tightrope between too much and too little, between a textbook for students on the one hand and an unduly popular presentation on the other. For help in maintaining my precarious balance and for many valuable criticisms and corrections I am deeply grateful to Dr Otto Edholm, Head of the Division of Human Physiology of the Medical Research Council, and Dr Raymond Hoffenberg, my successor in the Department of Endocrinology at New End Hospital, London.

Introduction

There are many so-called glands in the human body. Some, the lymphoid glands for instance, are properly known as lymphoid nodes and with their function we are not here concerned. The others are those which produce and discharge important chemical substances. These are divided into the *exocrine* glands which discharge their produce into ducts that lead them to their sites of activity; and the *endocrine* glands which discharge them into the blood stream, by way of which they reach every tissue, and indeed every cell of the body. It is with the second class only that this book will deal.

Endocrinology as a branch of medicine has had a troublesome career. A mere half-century ago it was not quite respectable. Too many smart-Alicks within and without the medical profession were, with great perspicacity but little knowledge, beginning to climb on to the band wagon.

The failure of orthodox doctors was largely due to the fact that endocrinology was a new science. Not much was known by the most learned. The less learned fell back on speculation and romance: 'the glands of destiny', 'we are governed by our glands', 'I don't know what is wrong – it must be something glandular', were phrases commonly heard. It was a quack's paradise, but so obviously so that in many hospitals physicians interested in endocrinology were looked upon askance. Twenty-five years ago there was no independent department of endocrinology in any London hospital.

Things are very different today. Hardly a hospital of any standing exists without an endocrinologist on its consultant staff. In many, a special department for endocrine disorders exists. A glance at the list of university professors of medicine, surgery, anatomy, physiology, paediatrics, gynaecology, and other medical subjects, shows that a high proportion of these eminent men began as endocrinologists who still encourage endocrine research in their departments. The Medical Research Council supports a number of eminent scientists in their research in the subject.

Endocrinology has shown itself to be the great integrator of medical science. It is a hard discipline. The endocrinologist must be physiologist, anatomist, biochemist, physicist, immunologist, geneticist, as well as physician. We have reached indeed a point when endocrinology as a speciality has ceased to exist. It is rather a torch always waiting to be shone into any dark corner of medicine. To change the metaphor, it is a tool that must be used in almost any medical research. No physician is much good unless he is an endocrinologist and equally no clinical endocrinologist is much good unless he is a general physician.

The reason for this is clear, though the permeance of endocrinology came as a surprise to those whose minds were attuned to the older concept of the ductless glands, which saw them in the same light as the glands with ducts, possessed of circumscribed and specific functions. They forgot that, though Nature often seems to be mad, there is usually a method in her madness. Why (they must have asked) should the ductless glands pour out their products into the blood stream in this apparently haphazard way to reach their targets only in a minute concentration and to waste themselves upon the desert air of indifferent tissues? Why should so extravagant a method have been adopted to lead the secretions of the ovaries to the near-by uterus when a duct would have served the purpose with so much greater economy? Is it not likely that every hormone, the name we have given to the secretions of the ductless glands, has, like insulin and thyroxine, a function in every cell? If this is so, every organ is subject to a certain extent to the activity of

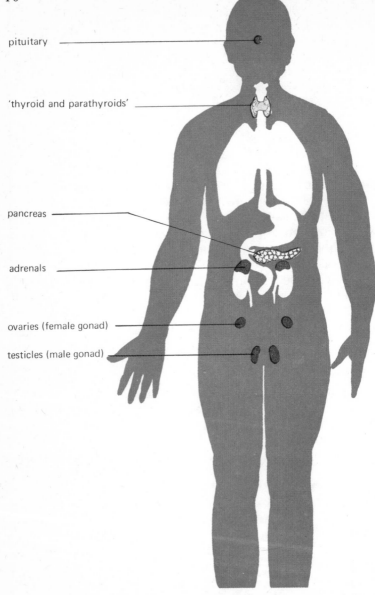

pituitary

'thyroid and parathyroids'

pancreas

adrenals

ovaries (female gonad)

testicles (male gonad)

The position of the endocrine glands.
The parathyroids, too small to be shown, lie
behind the outer margins of the thyroid.
In the unborn child, the ovaries and testicles are
low on each side of the pelvis but the testicles
usually descend into the scrotum before birth.

every hormone. Many such influences have come to light in recent years but many are still obscure.

Hughlings Jackson, the great neurologist of the nineteenth century, wrote: 'As scientific medical research goes on, there is greater specialisation of investigation, just as, in the development of society, there is that continually increasing specialisation called division of labour. This being so, all the more need is there that there should be greater integration, just as along with division of labour there is need for co-operation of labourers. . . . There is no harm in studying a special subject; the harm is in doing any kind of work with a narrow aim and a narrow mind.' The importance of endocrinology is in its integrative function in clinical medicine.

In 1941 I wrote: 'Endocrinology, formerly the study of easily recognised clinical conditions . . . has assumed a new shape, but one which grows from year to year more nebulous. It has become a part of all medicine. The integrative action of the endocrine glands in every function of the body through their control of metabolic processes has forced them upon the notice of every physician, wherever the focus of his special interest lies. . . . It is in the greater knowledge of the influence of the ductless glands on other systems that new advances are to be expected in the next few years. Research will be concerned less with the treatment of glandular disorders than with the function of those glands in the maintenance of the fine balance of the chemical reactions of health.'

It is a relatively simple matter to discover what hormones do. This is usually done by studying the effects on animals and human beings of total destruction, by surgery or disease, of the individual gland or those of the administration of extracts. It is far more difficult to find out how the hormones do what they do. We know for instance that thyroid hormone increases the metabolic rate, profoundly affects the function of the brain and autonomic nervous system, alters the balance of water and electrolytes, accelerates growth and the maturation of juvenile tissues, increases the production of milk, alters the pattern of metabolism of proteins, fats and carbohydrates, has far-reaching and important effects on the heart and blood vessels and increases the need for various vitamins. We know a lot about the interactions of the various hormones upon each other. We still know little about how these effects are produced but it is gradually becoming clearer that the essential action of hormones is upon the enzyme systems which control so many of the chemical reactions of the body.

1 Early history of the endocrines

The story of endocrinology begins with magic and some rather stuffy physicians would hold that it has never emerged from its humble origins. It is only in this century that many of our fellow human beings have ceased to eat the testicles of their enemies in the hope of emulating their sexual prowess. I have been offered bull's testicles in a restaurant in France by a waiter who clearly misjudged my reason for visiting his town. Thousands of years ago, the Chinese used the thyroid glands of animals to treat patients with thyroid deficiency, a substitution therapy more effective than the previous example.

Throughout history extracts of various organs have been the popular ingredients of medicines. The thymus was known to the Alexandrians in the third century before Christ. The thyroid, pineal and pituitary glands are said to have been described by Galen (b. AD 131). The adrenal glands were discovered by Eustachi in the sixteenth century. Diabetes is described in a Chinese book of the first century AD. In the seventeenth century the pharmacopoeias of the Royal College of Physicians contained a large number of nauseous substances comparable with the contents of the witches' cauldron in Shakespeare's *Macbeth*.

Until very recently pharmaceutical firms were marketing glandular and other tissue extracts almost equally bizarre, especially extracts of the sexual organs guaranteed to cure all those sexual deviations from the normal that were causing and continue to cause such distress and for which orthodox medicine could in the past do so little. Many doctors, more anxious than knowledgeable, were led astray by the commercial travellers into ill-conceived and useless attempts to help their patients by such means. When asked how a reputable firm could reconcile with its conscience the sale of prostatic extract as a cure for male sterility, impotence and 'neurasthenia', one of these was honest enough to reply that his firm was after all a commercial undertaking with a duty to its shareholders and could hardly withdraw from the market for scientific reasons a medicine still widely prescribed by doctors. At the same time, commercial 'endocrine clinics' were reaping rich rewards by giving useless injections to unfortunate patients who had achieved no benefit from their orthodox doctors.

All the same, serious research had continued. Though the Royal College continued to advocate its witch's brew, Thomas Willis of Oxford was introducing into medicine the concept of direct observation. He was at school in Oxford and went in 1636 to Christ Church in the lowly state of batteler or servant to one of the Canons, taking the degree of bachelor of medicine in 1646. He became Professor of Natural Philosophy at Oxford before moving to a successful practice in London in 1666. He described the system of arteries at the base of the brain still known as 'the circle of Willis' and was the first in modern times to diagnose diabetes mellitus by tasting the urine, although the Chinese knew about this by AD 700. He suspected that masculine characteristics were engendered by a substance secreted by the testes into the blood. His pupil Richard Lower, the confidant of Nell Gwynne, one of those who attended the death bed of Charles II, followed his master in hinting at the concept of internal secretion.

In the eighteenth century de Bordeu conceived the view that all tissues produce 'emanations' that entered the blood and excited distant effects. The idea gained ground in physiological circles, largely by the work of Dutch physicians such as Ruysch. John Hunter began an experimental approach by castrating cocks and observing the shrinkage of their combs, an observation followed up fifty years later by Berthold. But in general, endocrinology stood still until the great year of 1855, the year in which the modern science was born.

In that year were published the works of Claude Bernard of the Collège de France, Thomas Addison of Guy's Hospital, and Brown-Séquard of the National Hospital in London. Claude Bernard produced the concept of the ductless glands as the main integrative system of the body, contributing to what he called the fixity of the internal environment, the condition of the free life of the body, free to move through an ever-changing external environment; able to maintain almost constant internal conditions at the poles or in the tropics; maintaining a constant hydrogen-ion concentration while feeding on foods of varying acidity or alkalinity, a food and oxygen supply adjusted to the needs of every cell whatever the food supplied to the body as a whole, at rest and during exercise, at the bottom of a mine or at the top of a Himalayan peak. This great concept of Claude Bernard, adumbrated over a century ago, still rules our thoughts.

In the unicellular marine organism the constancy of the internal environment is easy to attain. The conditions within the cell are the same as those without, kept thus by the free passage of water and chemical substances in either direction through its thin surrounding membrane. As the organism becomes larger and multicellular some cells must of necessity become isolated from their marine environment. A mechanism had perforce to be evolved by which the conditions of the innermost cells could be equated with those at the periphery. The organism could no longer rely on osmosis, the free passage in and out, of the substances it needed and those it had to discard. With the development of an alimentary system by means of which the animal ingested food-stuffs of widely varying composition, the maintenance of the internal environment of the cells, now widely separated from the sea, became still more difficult, and the difficulty was enhanced when the animal left the sea for the rapidly changing external environment of the atmosphere. The development of the endocrine system made possible these adjustments.

In the same year, 1855, Thomas Addison described the effects of disease of the adrenal glands. That the adrenals produced an internal secretion had been postulated by Gulliver in 1840 but it was Addison who wrote the first description of an endocrine deficiency, which holds good to this day. Addison received little honour in his own country while alive, though in France Trousseau called adrenal deficiency 'Addison's disease', the name by which it is still known. He was grievously insulted and deeply hurt by the insults he received and five years later committed suicide.

Charles Edward Brown-Séquard was born in Mauritius in 1817 of mixed American and French ancestry. After graduating in medicine in Paris in 1846 he held professorial chairs there and in Harvard. He succeeded Claude Bernard as Professor of Experimental Medicine at the Collège de France. He ultimately became a physician at the National Hospital for Nervous Diseases in London, a Fellow of the Royal Society and of the Royal College of Physicians of London. Inspired by the work of Thomas Addison he removed the adrenal glands from an assortment of animals and showed that they were essential to life, though he held the erroneous view that the secretion of the adrenals exerted a 'detoxicating' influence, an idea which was not entirely abandoned until recent years.

Addison also inspired Sir Jonathan Hutchinson to collect clinical cases and post-mortem records. He expanded the concept of Brown-Séquard and believed, as we do today, that the ductless glands are organs whose secretions, discharged directly into the blood stream, affect the whole body.

We have now reached the point, a century ago, when the history of endocrinology becomes the history of the individual glands.

2 The endocrine company

The organisation of the endocrine system is not unlike that of a great commercial empire. Officially at the head of the company sits the chairman, who inhabits the frontal lobes of the brain, the seat of the intellect. It is not always a good thing to have an intellectual in such a position. Happily he rarely interferes with the day to day running of his companies. The disastrous effects of his occasional descents from Olympus will be described in a later chapter.

When all goes well, the management is in the hands of the very competent managing director, who resides in the *hypothalamus*. This small lump of tissue, the size of a damson, lies at the base of the brain immediately above the pituitary gland. It is connected by nervous tracts with the cerebral cortex above and by both nervous and humoral tracts with the pituitary below. The hypothalamus is the managing director not only of the endocrine system of glands but of the closely associated autonomic nervous system, which is the controlling influence over all the unconscious activities of the body.

This book is concerned mainly with the endocrine system but it is impossible to understand this without some idea of what the autonomic system does. This system is divided anatomically into two parts, the *sympathetic* and *parasympathetic* systems of nerves, both controlled by the hypothalamus. In vague general terms, the sympathetic system is brought into play in response to alarm, stress or anxiety, in preparation for 'fight or flight'. The response to emotion may be dramatic: it can be controlled by the intellect but usually is not, especially when higher cortical intellectual control is dulled by martial music, inspiring oratory or the various forms of brain-washing so admirably described by William Sargant in *The Battle for the Mind*. With little rational cause, the human, the so-called rational animal,

2·1 Section through the head to show the position of the pituitary gland.

19

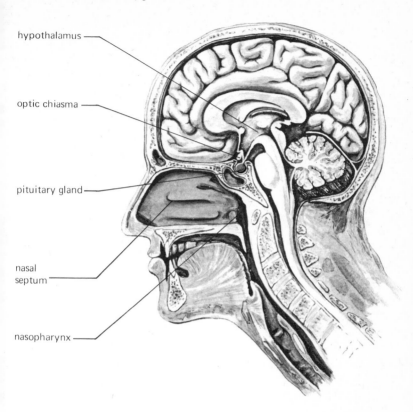

hypothalamus

optic chiasma

pituitary gland

nasal septum

nasopharynx

may be seen to 'stiffen the sinews, summon up the blood, disguise fair nature with hard-favoured rage' and in general to present an appearance reminiscent of a decorticated cat. These outward uncontrolled manifestations of emotion are accompanied by 'sympathetic' signs which have become the commonplaces of fiction, the sweating and pallor and dilated pupils of fear, the blushing of embarrassment, or the tears of uncontrolled laughter. The heart beats faster. The less urgent unconscious activities are suppressed, digestive processes are slowed, sexual activity is reduced, the desire to defaecate or to pass urine ceases, and the body is altogether brought to the alert as by an air raid siren.

The parasympathetic system has the opposite function. It is the system predominant in all peaceful functions. The heart is slowed, the movements of the bowels and bladder are stimulated, breathing is peaceful and slow, sexual activity becomes more efficient, sleep is more profound, the blood pressure falls.

In ordinary circumstances these opposite activities, both controlled by the hypothalamus, are nicely balanced. The balance is in part achieved by neural pathways, but the endocrine system also plays a part. We shall see later the part played by the adrenal medulla with its secretion of adrenaline and noradrenaline, the adrenal cortex with its secretion of cortisol, the pancreas with its secretion of insulin and the thyroid with its secretion of thyroxine.

In addition, the hypothalamus is concerned with the body's response to heat and cold, and with the metabolism of water, electrolytes, sugar and fat. It controls the appetite, growth, the sexual functions, the activity of the heart and blood vessels, respiration, digestion and sleep; indeed all those functions of the body that are usually beyond the control of conscious thought.

Many of these functions of the hypothalamus are performed by means of instructions issued to the endocrine glands through the medium of the pituitary gland.

It was formerly thought that the control of the pituitary gland by the hypothalamus was entirely neural. It is now realised that the control is a dual one, partly neural and partly humoral. Without this dual control, the connecting link between the higher centres of the brain and the other organs of the body, the mind would have no control over

2·2 The anatomy of the pituitary showing the nervous and vascular connections with the hypothalamus.

21

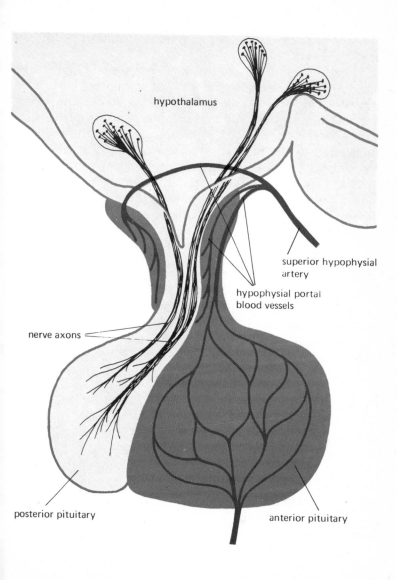

hypothalamus

superior hypophysial artery

hypophysial portal blood vessels

nerve axons

posterior pituitary

anterior pituitary

2·3 The central control of the endocrine system. The cerebral cortex has little or no control in health. The central control is in the hypothalamus which by its 'releasing factors' balances pituitary activity and is itself affected, by a feed-back mechanism, by the target endocrine glands. It controls also the autonomic nervous system which exercises some influence on the target glands, especially the adrenal medullae.

matter and the so-called psychosomatic disorders would not exist.

A vague idea of this control was expressed by Galen who believed that blood, containing 'vital spirits' (whatever was meant by this) travelled to the brain where these were transformed into 'animal spirits' (an equally incomprehensible term). The waste products of this change were, he believed, transferred to the pituitary and thence to the nasal cavity. Sir Richard Lower of Oxford dismissed this hypothesis and in 1670 expressed the view that any serum received by the pituitary from the brain was poured thence into the blood stream, and of course he hit the nail right on the head. There the matter rested until recent times when Marshall, Harris and others showed by modern techniques that electrical stimulation of the hypothalamus caused an increased discharge into the blood of many of the pituitary hormones later to be described. Hypothalamic damage was found to be followed by diminution of the output of some hormones and increase of others. Further experiments discounted the early idea of a purely neural connection between the hypothalamus and the pituitary and established the modern view that several 'releasing factors', humoral agents, are liberated from nerve endings into the capillaries which lie between the two organs and are carried into the anterior pituitary whose output of hormones they regulate. Moreover, the two hormones previously believed to be secreted by the posterior part of the pituitary, vasopressin and oxytocin, are now believed to be actually secreted in the hypothalamus and merely stored in the posterior lobe.

Releasing factors are now known that control the secretion of luteinising hormone (LH), follicle-stimulating hormone (FSH), thyrotrophic hormone (TSH), corticotrophin (ACTH)

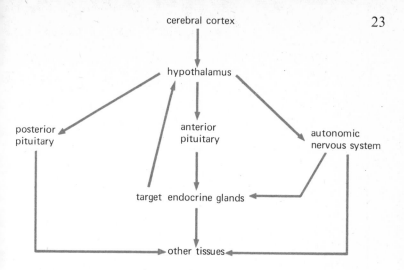

and growth hormone (GH or STH), all by the anterior pituitary lobe. The secretion of prolactin is less clear. It appears that the hypothalamus produces a substance which inhibits rather than stimulates its production. It has been shown that many things may influence the production of releasing factors from the hypothalamus, including stress, age, sex, the removal of 'target glands' such as the ovaries, testicles, adrenals and thyroid, treatment with the secretions of these 'target glands' and even the time of the year, the amount of light falling on the eyes, and the frequency of copulation.

But the influence of the hypothalamus on the endocrine system is like a constitutional monarchy. The hormones produced by the target glands affect the brain in many ways, as will be seen in later chapters. They also affect the secretion by the hypothalamus of its releasing factors. There is a servo-mechanism continuously at play, whereby a high concentration of a hormone from a target gland inhibits the production of the appropriate releasing factor, and therefore the production of the appropriate stimulating hormone by the anterior pituitary. Thus the secretion from the target gland is reduced and the situation made normal again. Though

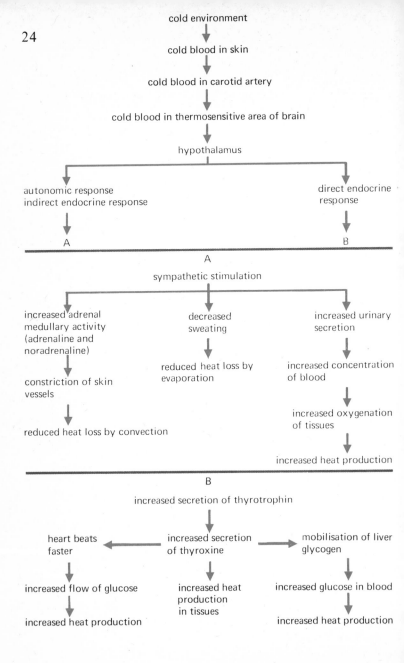

2·4 The response to cold.
The response of the intact healthy body
to cold is a very complicated one.
It is a good example of the way in which
the hormones and the automatic nervous
system work in perpetual partnership.

25

in 'normal' circumstances this feed-back mechanism is continuously active, it may be upset by disease and by the many environmental influences already mentioned.

But though it is with the strictly endocrine regulation by the hypothalamus that we are chiefly concerned, it would be wrong to omit consideration of its other functions, for they are closely interlocked.

The hypothalamus is the organ most closely concerned with the body's reaction to cold and heat. The first reaction to a fall in external temperature is brought about by cooling of the blood in the skin. The cooled peripheral blood, mixing with the general circulation, produces a minute fall in the temperature of the blood in the carotid arteries which supply the brain. Here there is a thermosensitive area which passes the message on to the hypothalamus. An impulse then passes through the sympathetic nerves to the medullae (the inner parts of the adrenal glands) which respond by an increased production of its hormones. These constrict the peripheral circulation, thus decreasing heat loss from the surface of the body. The sympathetic impulse also increases the secretion of thyroxine by the thyroid. The rate of oxidation in all cells of the body is thus increased, a process like turning up the gas in a central heating stove. It mobilises from the liver a substance, glycogen, which is the precursor of glucose, and provides the additional fuel needed for the increased oxidation. It speeds the heart and transmits the glucose more rapidly to every cell. The secretion of urine is increased, with consequent concentration of the blood. The secretion of sweat is decreased, so that less heat is lost by evaporation. Respiration is affected, so that more oxygen becomes available. After a 'heat debt' of more than nine hundred calories has been incurred, shivering begins and in

anterior part
of hypothalamus
responds to blood
ions and regulates
production and
release of antidiuretic
hormone (vasopressin)

antidiuretic hormone
descends nerve fibres
and is picked up by
capillaries of
neurohypophysis

ACTH

antidiuretic
hormone (ADH
or vasopressin)

antidiuretic hormone makes
distal convoluted tubule permeable
to water and thus permits it to be
reabsorbed along with actively
reabsorbed salt

antidiuretic hormone makes
collecting tubule permeable to
water, permitting its reabsorption
due to high osmolality of renal
medulla

2·5 The control of water
metabolism, another example
of the partnership between
the hormones and the automatic
nervous system. The object is to
keep the constitution of the
tissue fluid constant and as
near as possible to our
ancestors' marine environment.

14 to 18 litres reabsorbed
daily under influence
of antidiuretic hormone,
resulting in 1 to 2 litres
of urine in 24 hours

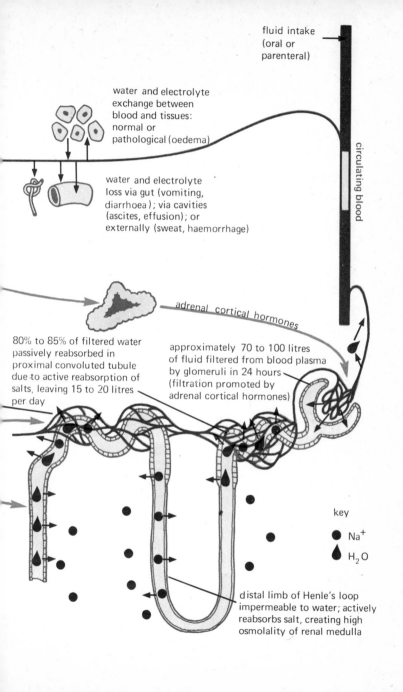

fluid intake (oral or parenteral)

circulating blood

water and electrolyte exchange between blood and tissues: normal or pathological (oedema)

water and electrolyte loss via gut (vomiting, diarrhoea); via cavities (ascites, effusion); or externally (sweat, haemorrhage)

adrenal cortical hormones

80% to 85% of filtered water passively reabsorbed in proximal convoluted tubule due to active reabsorption of salts, leaving 15 to 20 litres per day

approximately 70 to 100 litres of fluid filtered from blood plasma by glomeruli in 24 hours (filtration promoted by adrenal cortical hormones)

key

Na^+

H_2O

distal limb of Henle's loop impermeable to water; actively reabsorbs salt, creating high osmolality of renal medulla consequence more oxygen is used. None of these reactions occurs in an animal whose hypothalamus has been removed.

In the converse condition of excessive ambient heat, the adaptation of the body is achieved by increased sweating and consequent loss of heat by evaporation, and by dilatation of the blood vessels of the skin and consequent loss of heat by convection. By way of the thyroid, the general metabolic rate is lowered; the 'stove' is turned down.

Sleep is regulated by the hypothalamus. Pathological somnolence is seen in diseases like encephalitis (sleepy sickness) and in other conditions in which the hypothalamus is affected. Severe damage to the hypothalamus accounts for the coma of head injuries, in which endocrine abnormalities such as high blood sugar and disturbances of water metabolism also occur.

The output of water is under hypothalamic control. It takes place in part from the skin and lungs and in part from the kidneys. The glomeruli of the kidneys, by a process of filtration, allow the passage outwards into the tubules of a fluid which is identical with blood plasma without its protein and fat, these being retained in the blood. The function of the tubules is the controlled reabsorption of water, the control resting with vasopressin, the antidiuretic hormone secreted by the hypothalamus and stored in the posterior pituitary lobe. Damage to the hypothalamus, to the connecting links with the pituitary or to the posterior pituitary results in a failure of the tubules to reabsorb water and a condition known clinically as diabetes insipidus, in which the patient continuously produces large quantities of urine and suffers in consequence an agonising thirst and disturbed sleep. An opposite condition known as diabetes tenuifluus is occasionally seen in hypothalamic disorders. The output of the antidiuretic hormone, like other hypothalamic activities, is subject to many environmental influences. Anxiety especially may increase it and produce water retention within the body.

The superior control of carbohydrate metabolism is also a hypothalamic duty. The hypothalamus performs this duty in several ways, which will become clearer when the functions of the anterior pituitary hormones are discussed, for these are the main channels through which its influence is exerted. Excessive (hyperglycaemic) and deficient (hypoglycaemic) levels of sugar in the blood are often found after operations and injuries at the base of the brain and in patients with tumours, haemorrhage and meningitis in this region. Part of the hypothalamus (the paraventricular nucleus) undergoes degeneration when the pancreas is removed and this has been found in cases of death from diabetes mellitus. Extreme degrees of hypoglycaemia have been found to follow removal of the hypothalamus and of hyperglycaemia after removal of the pancreas, whereas if both are removed the animal survives with, however, a diminished capacity for adaptation.

It has long been known that the hypothalamus has a control over the appetite. Patients with tumours at the base of the brain may develop voracious appetites and become enormously obese. Experimental damage to various parts of the hypothalamus has located the exact site of the appetite-regulating centre in experimental animals. The significance of the appetite centre in human medicine will be made clear in the chapters on obesity and on behaviour.

The hypothalamus, then, is the area of the brain in which the real control of the endocrine system is situated. The pituitary, long known as 'the conductor of the endocrine orchestra' has lost its full primacy, but it remains the most important of the endocrine glands.

Part 1

Hormones
gland by gland

3 The pituitary gland

As late as 1889, Macalister, Professor of Anatomy at Cambridge, described the pituitary gland as 'the rudiment of an archaic sense organ'. Known to exist since the time of Galen, this minute but potent organ has had many fanciful functions ascribed to it. Scientific research began only with Harvey Cushing in 1905 and its important position in the endocrine system has established itself only in the last forty years, owing to the work of so many investigators that to mention names must be invidious. Nevertheless it is justifiable to mention such pioneers as Greving, Roussy, Mossinger, Harris, and Zuckerman and, in the clinical field, Marie, Simmonds, Sheehan, Frölich, Langdon-Brown and Crooke.

The pituitary gland is a small organ about the size of a hazel nut lying in a bony cave, the so-called sella turcica, at the base of the brain. It consists of three parts, the anterior, posterior, and median lobes. The anterior lobe is made of recognisably glandular (epithelial) tissue, but the posterior lobe is made of nervous tissue, which was often a sore point in histological discussion. How could a structure consisting of nervous tissue behave like a gland? In the first place, it does not. In the second place, the hypothalamus, also consisting of nervous tissue, emphatically does. The pars intermedia, lying between the two lobes, is, like the anterior lobe, epithelial in structure. It appears to have a function largely concerned with the regulation of pigments in most animals, but its importance, if any, in human physiology is still obscure. The whole gland is connected with the hypothalamus above it by blood vessels and by nerves of the autonomic system.

The anterior pituitary

The anterior pituitary is necessary for life. It produces the three gonadotrophic hormones, which regulate the sexual functions of both men and women, the corticotrophic hormone which controls the adrenals, the thyrotrophic hormone which controls the thyroid, and the growth hormone.

The gonadotrophic hormones The three gonadotrophic hormones are called the follicle stimulating hormone (FSH), the luteinising hormone (LH) and luteotrophin or prolactin. These hormones are proteins. The follicle stimulating hormone (FSH) is released from the anterior pituitary in response to a hypothalamic releasing factor (FSH-RF). Its main concern is the production of the ovarian follicles in the woman and of spermatozoa in the man. The luteinising hormone is chiefly concerned with the production of corpora lutea in the woman and of the male hormone testosterone in the man. The functions of the follicle stimulating and luteinising hormones will be described in detail in later chapters.

The third gonadotrophic hormone of the anterior pituitary is luteotrophin or prolactin. It has important actions on the mammary gland, stimulates the pigeon's crop, has some general growth promoting activities and in addition has effects which somewhat resemble those of luteinising hormone. It has never been isolated in human beings and some authorities doubt whether it exists in them. It may be the same as growth hormone. If it does exist its main activity is to collaborate with oestradiol and progesterone in the production of milk, the ovarian hormones causing growth of the mammary glands but at the same time keeping the production of prolactin in check. The fall in ovarian hormones at

34

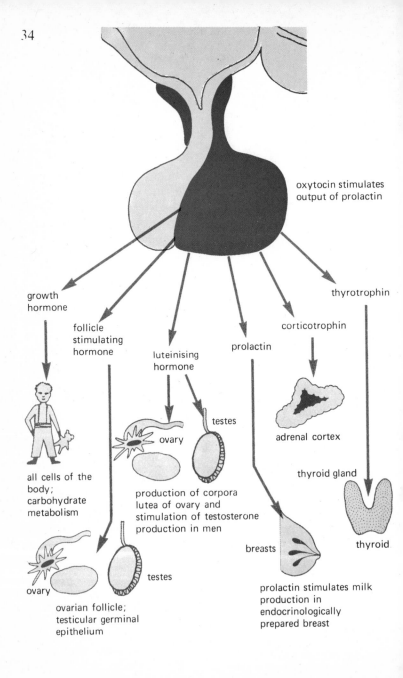

3·1 The sites of action of the
anterior pituitary hormones.

35

parturition allows the pituitary to produce prolactin and lactation begins. However, other hormones are necessary, as we shall see later, for the efficient production of milk.

The growth hormone The growth hormone acts directly on the tissues of the body without the intervention of any target gland. Its essential activity is the promotion of protein anabolism – the building up of the tissues by an increase in the use of protein for this purpose at the expense of its use in the production of energy. The removal of the pituitary of an animal or its destruction by disease in a child causes cessation of growth: an excessive production by a tumour of the pituitary causes the child to become a giant. Growth of the long bones cannot continue when they have fully matured and the ends have united with the shafts and excessive growth in the adult occurs only in other tissues, producing the disease of acromegaly. Growth hormone antagonises the action of insulin and some acromegalics become diabetic, although some do not because their pancreases are capable of making good the deficiency.

The growth hormone is derived from cells in the anterior pituitary which stain pink when treated with the dye eosin and are therefore called eosinophil cells. There is a race of dwarf mice which possesses no eosinophil cells; the mice can be made to grow normally by treatment with growth hormone. Conversely, it is a tumour of the eosinophil cells which causes gigantism and acromegaly.

Dwarfism, however, has many other causes that will be discussed in chapter 10.

The growth hormone is also concerned with carbohydrate metabolism. Its production is stimulated by a low level of glucose in the blood (hypoglycaemia) and suppressed by a

3·2 The effects of anxiety on water balance. The course of events was established in dogs by Verney. It is often forgotten that an identical course of events can occur in human beings.

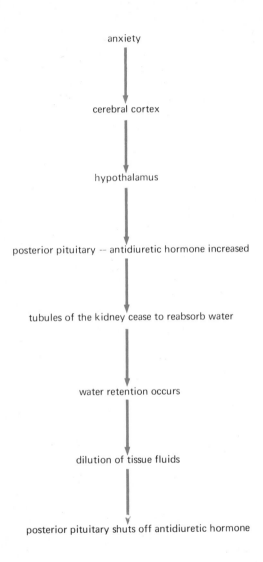

anxiety

↓

cerebral cortex

↓

hypothalamus

↓

posterior pituitary – antidiuretic hormone increased

↓

tubules of the kidney cease to reabsorb water

↓

water retention occurs

↓

dilution of tissue fluids

↓

posterior pituitary shuts off antidiuretic hormone

high one. Diabetic children are therefore small if their disease is not well treated. Another factor that increases the secretion of growth hormone is stress, including violent exercise and anxiety. It is possible that these are responsible for the fact that boys in the expensive public schools in England, playing games daily and subjected to a discipline unknown in free state schools, tended to be taller.

So far supplies of growth hormone are difficult to obtain, for only human growth hormone is effective in the human being. The time will undoubtedly come when it will be synthesised and available then for the treatment of all dwarfs and under-grown children whose small size is due to pituitary deficiency. It is unlikely to be effective, at any rate to the same extent, in dwarfism due to other causes.

The thyrotrophic hormone The thyrotrophic hormone (TSH) or thyrotrophin controls the activity of the thyroid gland in health by a nicely balanced servo-mechanism. By way of the hypothalamus and the appropriate releasing factor, too high an activity of the thyroid shuts off its own steam; too low an activity increases the pressure. This mechanism sometimes fails in ill health. In thyrotoxicosis, for instance, an abnormal globulin in the blood known as the long-acting thyroid stimulator (LATS) stimulates the thyroid despite the shutting down of the production of thyrotrophin. In myxoedema, the utmost efforts of the pituitary fail to stimulate the sluggish thyroid gland.

The relationship of the pituitary to the thyroid is perhaps the best known example of the endocrine servo-relationship. It has been suspected ever since, in the last century, it was found that the pituitary was enlarged in cretins, who were early known to be suffering from a congenital thyroid deficiency. The experiments of P.E.Smith and H.M.Evans in the 1920s established the relationship: they found atrophy of the thyroid after removal of the pituitary and its restoration to normal by treatment with pituitary extract. Later workers showed depression of the thyroid stimulating activity of the pituitary by the administration of thyroid hormone and its stimulation by removal of the thyroid or depression of thyroid activity by drugs. The servo-relationship works at an astonishing speed. Geoffrey Harris, whose experiments have cast a flood of light over the whole hypothalamic-pituitary-target organ mechanism, has shown that inhibition of thyroid activity by thyroxine, the thyroid hormone, or by stress, or its activation by exposure to cold, take place in two to four hours. Nevertheless thyroid activity continues, albeit at a low level, in animals lacking hypothalamus and pituitary, just as a well-tuned engine will continue to tick over slowly in neutral with no application by the driver of accelerator or brake. The mechanism is still incompletely understood, but there is reason to believe that other factors, such as the peripheral disposal of thyroxine and the effect upon it of food intake, may be involved. We shall discuss later the effects on the servo-mechanism of pregnancy, of drugs and of stress.

It was formerly held by many workers that in thyroid disorders the excessive or deficient production of thyroxine depended upon the level of production of thyrotrophin and therefore, by later implication, upon the action of the hypothalamic thyrotrophin-releasing factor. It now seems probable that this neat control operates perfectly only in health and that other factors exercise a more potent controlling activity in disease. The mysterious long-acting thyroid stimulating factor (LATS) enters the field here.

The adrenocorticotrophic hormone The adrenocorticotrophic hormone (ACTH) or corticotrophin is perhaps the best known of the products of the anterior pituitary, largely because it has shouldered its way before the others into clinical practice. Its function is the regulation of the cortex of the adrenal glands. The rate of secretion by the adrenal cortex of cortisol and corticosterone is under its sole control: that of aldosterone is more complex (see chapter 5).

However, it has other effects. In large doses it influences animals without their adrenal glands. It lowers their blood-sugar, increases the release of fatty acids from adipose tissue (and hence increases the level of free fatty acids in the blood) and increases liver fat. These actions may have no significance in health, though it is always unwise to assume that any action of any hormone is unimportant. Of known importance is the effect of corticotrophin on pigmentation. The patient with Addison's disease, due to disease of the adrenals, usually has a dark skin. The patient whose adrenals have been removed because of Cushing's disease, in which they are overactive, or in an attempt to delay the progress of cancer, develops a pigmentation deep enough in some instances to suggest African or Asian heredity. Studies of the level of circulating corticotrophin suggest that it is this hormone *per se* that produces the darkening of the skin but the possible contribution of melanotrophic hormone from the intermediate lobe of the pituitary remains unsettled (see chapter 19).

The posterior pituitary

The posterior pituitary is anatomically and physiologically an extension by way of the pituitary stalk of the hypo-

3·3 The sites of action of the posterior pituitary hormones.

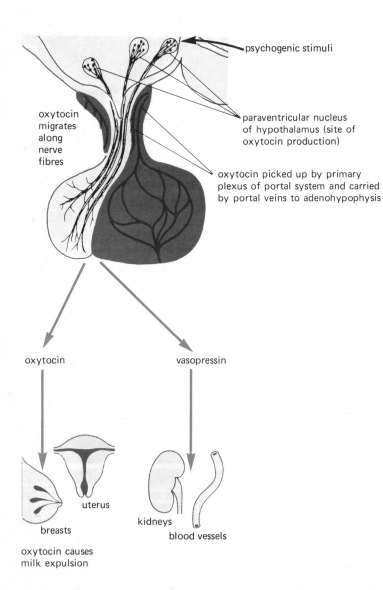

psychogenic stimuli

oxytocin migrates along nerve fibres

paraventricular nucleus of hypothalamus (site of oxytocin production)

oxytocin picked up by primary plexus of portal system and carried by portal veins to adenohypophysis

oxytocin

vasopressin

breasts

uterus

kidneys

blood vessels

oxytocin causes milk expulsion

thalamus. From it may be extracted two hormones formerly believed to be manufactured in the pituitary, but now known to be produced in the hypothalamus and merely stored there. The two hormones are known as vasopressin, or antidiuretic hormone (ADH), and oxytocin.

Vasopressin Vasopressin has a dual function. It stimulates plain or unstriped muscles, the muscles of the body outside the conscious control of the mind, such as those of the blood vessels, bronchi, and intestinal tract. It also controls the reabsorption of water by the renal tubules, so that when present in excess water retention occurs, whereas when it is deficient too little water is reabsorbed and an excessive output of urine occurs, an action already described in the previous chapter. Its action on the blood vessels causes pallor, a slow pulse, and a decrease in oxygen consumption and in the cardiac output of blood. From the point of view of clinical medicine the second is the more important action, for it is closely controlled by the higher centres of the brain and by the emotional state of the individual, fear and anxiety producing an increase in the secretion of antidiuretic hormone and consequent retention of water in the tissues of the body. The secretion of antidiuretic hormone is controlled by the so-called osmoreceptors in the hypothalamus. These centres are very sensitive to the degree of dilution of the tissue fluids. Loss of water from the body causes a rise in the osmotic pressure of the blood, an increased output of antidiuretic hormone and therefore a decreased output of urine. Conversely dilution of the blood causes a decrease in antidiuretic hormone and an increased output of urine. The process is a beautiful example of the action of the endocrine system in maintaining the constancy of the internal environment

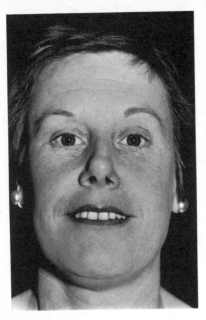

but, like most endocrine actions, it is not an entirely autonomous one. The process depends in part on the adrenal glands. Failure to secrete antidiuretic hormone causes an increase in urinary secretion only when these are working satisfactorily. If the adrenals are destroyed, as in Addison's disease, or if they are insufficiently stimulated, as when the anterior pituitary is diseased, the increased output of urine does not occur.

Oxytocin The second hormone stored by the posterior pituitary is oxytocin. Its important function is to cause contraction of the uterus. Small doses cause a slight increase in the rate of spontaneous contractions, larger doses increasing both rate and strength. However, for such an effect to occur, other hormones are necessary. The uterus of an immature animal or one from which the ovaries have been removed is quite insensitive to oxytocin. If in such animals the oestrogenic hormone of the ovaries is administered the uterus

3·4 Left Simmonds' disease, a form of panhypopituitarism, before and after treatment. Note the improvement in facial contours, the quality of the skin and hair, and the expression.

3·5 Right Acromegaly, due to a pituitary tumour. Note the coarse features, protuberance of the nose and chin and the spade-like hands. The asymmetry of the face, an uncommon feature, is well shown.

becomes sensitive. The other ovarian hormone, progesterone, depresses its sensitivity. Probably for this reason, the sensitivity varies throughout the menstrual cycle and gradually increases during pregnancy.

Oxytocin has an important action on the breasts, causing the milk to be squeezed out of the alveoli into the ducts leading to the nipple. It causes a transient fall in blood pressure by dilating the vessels in the limbs, but the significance of this activity in the maintenance of health is still unknown.

The median lobe

The melanocyte stimulating hormone is present in the pituitary gland of human beings and of all mammals and amphibians so far investigated. Its most important known action is in amphibians in which it expands the melanocytes, the pigment-bearing cells of their skin. It causes darkening of the skin in human beings, probably by stimulating the production of the black pigment melanin. This activity will be discussed in greater detail in chapter 18. It is produced in greater quantity in pregnancy, when it is the probable cause of the pigmentation of the nipples and the appearance in some women of a patchy pigmentation of the face known as chloasma. It is partly the cause of the darkening of the skin in Addison's disease, and its absence causes the pale skin of patients with pituitary deficiency.

Too much and too little

Each of the pituitary hormones may be produced in a quantity too great or too small for normal health. Too great a secretion of the gonadotrophic and thyrotrophic hormones is of no known importance in practical medicine, but their deficiency is otherwise. Without the former the ovaries of women and the testicles of men fail to produce their essential hormones. In children, sexual development does not occur. Women fail to menstruate, men become impotent and both become infertile. Without a sufficiency of the latter, the thyroid functions poorly and the effects of thyroid deficiency to be described in chapter 6 soon become manifest. Too little corticotrophin leads to adrenal deficiency (see chapter 4). Deficiency of growth hormone shows itself only in children, in whom growth ceases. These deficiencies are most often seen in Sheehan's disease. In this condition, the shock of severe haemorrhage after childbirth causes spasm of the small arteries supplying blood to the pituitary, with consequent necrosis and diminution or actual extinction of pituitary function. There follow all the effects of gonadal, thyroid and adrenal deficiency to be described later. Similar effects may follow rarer diseases of the pituitary due to tumours or infections.

Too high an excretion of the gonadotrophins and thyrotrophin is not a recognised cause of disease, but two of the best known endocrine disorders are caused by an excessive secretion of growth hormone, usually due to a tumour of the acidophil cells. If this happens in childhood, an excessive growth of the long bones occurs and the unfortunate sufferer grows to gigantic height, in the case of 'the Alton giant' to almost nine feet. Such growth, as will be explained later, can occur only while the bones are still immature. Later, when the long bones have become incapable of further growth, the disease of acromegaly occurs. The excessive growth affects chiefly the soft tissues and the bones of the face, hands and feet, producing a most bizarre appearance.

Overproduction of corticotrophin produces the well-known disorder known as Cushing's disease: this will be described in chapter 4.

4 The adrenal cortex

The adrenal glands sit like hats on the upper poles of the kidneys and consist of a central *medulla* within the *cortex* or outer bark. The cortex is essential to life. It is a confusing organ that produces a very large number of hormones. About thirty have been isolated but most of these are either intermediate substances or breakdown products. Some, the androgenic, oestrogenic and progestogenic hormones will be described in the chapters that deal with the gonadal (testicular and ovarian) hormones. All of these hormones are steroids. They consist of variations on the theme of pregnane but they differ widely in their functions. They are concerned with sex, dealt with in a later chapter, sugar metabolism, salt and water metabolism, and resistance to stress. The main ones are hydrocortisone or cortisol, concerned chiefly with reaction to stress and with sugar metabolism, and aldosterone, concerned only with salt metabolism.

The corticosteroids, as all these hormones are called, are synthesised in the adrenal cortex, originally from acetate and thence by way of cholesterol. It would be tedious to trace in detail the complicated chemical pathway that cholesterol must follow in its conversion by enzymes into the finished hormone. Briefly, cholesterol is present in almost all tissues of the body but is especially concentrated in the cortex of the adrenal glands. The first change, which is regulated by corticotrophin secreted by the anterior pituitary, is the conversion of cholesterol into pregnenolone by the splitting off of part of its molecule. Thereafter corticotrophin plays no part, further changes being regulated by enzymes already present in the gland. These convert pregnenolone partly into progesterone and partly into 17-hydroxy-pregnenolone, and thence by complicated pathways, not all completely clear, into the final products. Like thyroxine, the corticosteroids circulate in the body in combination with proteins, but exert their physiological activity only when free from these.

The hormones affecting sugar metabolism, of which we may take cortisol as the type, are known as glucocorticoids. They have as their main activity the regulation of the storage in the liver of glycogen, the raw product from which glucose is derived. When they are present in excess, not only is more glycogen deposited under the influence of cortisol but more glucose is formed from protein, a process known as gluco-neogenesis. In addition the peripheral action of insulin is reduced. This is why in deficiency of the adrenals the level of sugar in the blood may fall dangerously low. Less sugar is formed, less is stored, and more is used. Conversely when the adrenals overact, as in Cushing's disease, too much protein is broken down and converted into glucose. Thus the protein structures of the body are weakened: the skin, for instance, loses its elasticity and the bones are weakened. Growth is inhibited. Too much sugar circulates (steroid diabetes), too little sugar is used, and too much is stored as fat. Cortisol has an effect also in the regulation of salt and water metabolism, though this is less pronounced than that of aldosterone. In excess it causes an excessive loss of potassium due to its liberation from protein and to diminished reabsorption by the tubules of the kidneys. At the same time an excessive amount of sodium is retained. The effect of cortisol on water balance is complicated: its influence is directed towards the prevention of either water retention or dehydration. On the one hand it increases the rate of filtration of the glomeruli of the kidneys and thus produces a diuresis. On the other hand by causing sodium retention it has the opposite effect, for water must be retained to maintain the constancy of the sodium content of the body fluids. A fine balance in health is

**glucocorticoids
(cortisol)**

**mineralocorticoids
(aldosterone)**

**androgens
(testosterone)**

4·1 Chemical formulae of steroid hormones. Apparently small differences in structure profoundly influence physiological activity.

4·2 Cushing's syndrome, due to adrenal overactivity. Note, before treatment, the round hairy and dusky face, the coarse skin with acne spots and the obesity. All were corrected (far right) by the removal of both adrenal glands.

thus maintained, but in adrenal deficiency (Addison's disease) there is a failure to excrete a water load that can be corrected only by glucocorticoids.

The glucocorticoids are the bulwark of the body against stress. Although his views have been hotly contested and some have been shown to be erroneous, it is to Hans Selye that the credit is due for the great advance of knowledge in this quarter that has taken place in the last twenty years. In response to a great variety of stresses, such as surgical or accidental injury, emotion, hypoglycaemia and infection, there is a rise in the production of glucocorticoids. This response involves the whole 'axis', from the higher centres of the brain, by way of the hypothalamus, anterior pituitary and adrenal cortex. It has been demonstrated in many circumstances, such as surgical shock, pain, intense emotional stress, anxiety and even excessive noise. Conversely in one experiment the viewing of a Walt Disney film caused a reduction of the glucocorticoids in the blood to unmeasurable levels!

The glucocorticoids are clinically of the greatest importance in dealing with many diseases. They have an important anti-inflammatory effect which may be beneficial, as when they are used in the treatment of rheumatoid arthritis, or they may be very dangerous. The danger arises from the fact that the phenomena of inflammation are unpleasant but necessary to recovery, and that even symptoms are valuable in drawing attention to the presence of disease. Under the influence of cortisone given, for instance, in the treatment of rheumatoid arthritis, a man may die of pneumonia without realising that there is anything wrong in his chest. The glucocorticoids have a valuable action in combating allergic reactions, as we shall see in later chapters.

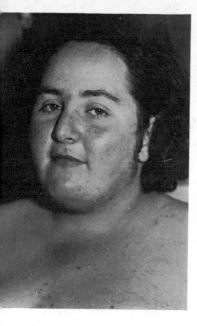 

The mineralocorticoid activity of the adrenal glands is, as we have seen, part of the function of the glucocorticoid hormones, mainly cortisol. However it is more importantly the function of aldosterone. The mineralocorticoid activity of aldosterone is fifty times that of cortisol. Aldosterone is certainly the senior partner in any partnership that may exist. In its absence, as in total destruction of the adrenal glands, there is so excessive a loss of sodium from the body that life is impossible. The story of its discovery by Tait, Simpson and Grundy in 1952 is a fascinating one. An extract of adrenal tissue, after all known steroids had been removed, still showed a life-prolonging action in animals whose adrenals had been extirpated, but the substance responsible for this remained unidentified until the new method of chromatography was applied to the problem. Within an astonishingly short space of time a new steroid had been identified, crystallised, characterised, and finally synthesised. It was soon found to be present in excess in the urine of patients

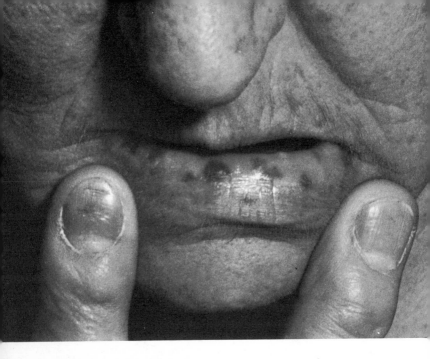

with nephrosis and congestive heart failure. Even before this it had been discovered that the adrenal produced, from just one layer of its cells, the zona glomerulosa, a powerful salt-retaining hormone. Within a year of its discovery, it became clear that this was aldosterone. Moreover it was shown that, unlike other adrenal steroids, it is not completely under pituitary control. The zona glomerulosa does not atrophy, as the rest of the adrenal does, when the pituitary is removed. It increases in size in sodium deprivation and decreases in potassium deprivation. The clinician has long realised that in pituitary deficiency the glucocorticoid activity of the adrenal is depressed because of the absence of corticotrophin, whereas the salt metabolism is less affected.

Changes in the rate of production of aldosterone result from changes in the salt metabolism of the body. The control by which these changes are accomplished is less obvious. The original idea that corticotrophin exercised no effect at all was

4·3 Addison's disease.
The patchy pigmentation of the
lips is a characteristic sign.

53

proved wrong, but it is probably a minor one. The immediate controlling factor appears to be humoral rather than nervous, but the source of the 'humour' is still a matter for controversy.

Although aldosterone has a slight activity resembling that of the glucocorticoids, its essential action is to cause retention of sodium and depletion of potassium. When, as in Conn's syndrome, an aldosterone-producing tumour is present, the low potassium level causes paralysis of muscles; the high sodium level causes fluid retention and a high blood pressure.

The various activities of the adrenal cortical hormones are explored in greater detail in later chapters.

Too much and too little

We have seen that the production of cortisol is under pituitary control. Without pituitary stimulation the adrenal glands remain inactive and are unable to react to the stresses of life. Even between stresses the patient is weak, abnormally fatigued, with a poor appetite, nausea and vomiting. Constipation or diarrhoea and muscular pain are common. When the disease is due to atrophy of the adrenal glands, an example of 'autoimmune disease' or their destruction by tuberculosis, the deficiency of cortisol stimulates an excessive production of corticotrophin and a brown pigmentation of the skin (see chapter 19). Before the discovery of cortisone the disease was invariably fatal.

An excessive production of adrenal cortical hormones, due either to too much corticotrophin or to an active adrenal tumour, causes the disease known as Cushing's syndrome in which all the functions of cortisol are present to an abnormal extent. Too much protein is converted into glucose: the bones and skin are weak for lack of it and the glucose circulates in the blood (steroid diabetes) and is stored as fat. Salt is retained in the tissues and the blood pressure rises. The loss of protein from the bones especially of the spine makes them subject to spontaneous fracture. Its loss from the skin causes undue transparency, easy bruising and extreme fragility.

Aldosterone may also be produced to an excessive extent, usually as a result of a tumour. In this disorder, often called Conn's syndrome, the excessive retention of sodium causes high blood pressure and severe headache. The level of potassium falls and produces muscular weakness. Kidney damage ultimately ensues.

5 The adrenal medulla

The adrenal medulla, although it lies within the outer bark of the adrenal cortex like a kernel within a nut, is physiologically an entirely separate organ. It is a part of the autonomic nervous system and it produces two hormones (chemically known as catecholamines) called adrenaline and noradrenaline. The existence of adrenaline was first suspected in 1894 by a Harrogate clinician named Oliver who voiced his suspicions to his friend Schäfer, then Professor of Physiology at University College in London. Schäfer and Benjamin Moore, later to be my teacher at Oxford, followed up Oliver's suspicions and demonstrated in adrenal extracts a substance that dramatically raised the blood pressure of anaesthetised animals. This substance, now known as adrenaline, was isolated in 1901 by Takamine and by Aldrich, the first hormone ever isolated. It was synthesised by Stolz and by Dakin in 1904, and a series of brilliant researches, especially those of Sir Henry Dale, who died only recently at the age of 93, led not only to an accurate knowledge of the actions of adrenaline but to the discovery of its near relation noradrenaline, and to the concept of the close partnership between the autonomic and endocrine systems of the body.

Unlike the hormones of the adrenal cortex, the catecholamines are not steroids. Though so closely alike chemically they have very different activities. They can be demonstrated in many different tissues apart from the adrenals, notably in the so-called chromaffin tissue elsewhere in the abdomen, the vas deferens, heart, salivary glands and spleen. A third hormone, dopamine, has recently been found in the medulla and in many other organs, notably in nervous tissue. At one time thought to be a stage in the manufacture of adrenaline and noradrenaline it is now suspected of having an important task of its own.

Adrenaline is chiefly a vasodilator, a substance which dilates the arteries. It causes the blood pressure to rise by increasing the output of blood from the heart. Noradrenaline on the other hand is in general a vasoconstrictor and hardly affects the cardiac output. Both raise the blood sugar by mobilising glycogen from the liver, though the action of adrenaline in this respect is greater. Both dilate the coronary arteries of the heart.

The output of adrenaline is continuous, but as we have seen earlier it is suddenly increased in any situation of stress, anxiety, anger or terror. It is in this situation that we see most clearly the partnership between the endocrine and nervous tissues. The output of adrenaline from the adrenal medulla is increased by the action of acetylcholine liberated when the splanchnic nerve in the abdomen is stimulated.

It had previously been naively thought that the sympathetic nerves liberated adrenaline with resultant characteristically sympathetic effects and that the parasympathetic nerves liberated acetylcholine with resultant characteristically parasympathetic effects. The discovery by Dale that some sympathetic nerves liberated acetylcholine, notably the splanchnic nerves to the adrenals and the nerves to the sweat glands, led him to a new classification of the autonomic system. He proposed that autonomic nerves liberating adrenaline should be called adrenergic and those liberating acetylcholine cholinergic, thus cutting straight across the old anatomical division.

Much controversy arose about the part played by the adrenal medulla in the response to stress. How much was due to the activity of the hypothalamus ordering the release of adrenaline by adrenergic nerves, how much to the effects of adrenaline released from the adrenals? It was found that the

5·1 Overleaf The production and physiological effects of the hormones of the adrenal medulla. Emotional impulses, acting by way of the hypothalamus and the autonomic nervous system, stimulate the synthesis of adrenaline and noradrenaline in the adrenal medulla. These, circulating in the blood, profoundly affect the various tissues of the body.

application of adrenaline to nerve endings was ineffective in organs cut off from their usual nerve supply, but the organs themselves were unduly sensitive, and nicotine, which paralyses the sympathetic ganglia, did not inhibit the action of adrenaline on the whole organ. It may be guessed from this that in ordinary circumstances the behaviour of organs is controlled by the adrenaline released by the nerves supplying them and that in emergency the extra weight of the medullary adrenaline is thrown in in support. Cannon showed that stimulation of the splanchnic nerves of whole cats caused an increase in heart rate of an average of twenty-nine beats per minute. After removal of the adrenals an increase still occurred, but only of six beats per minute. The substance responsible for this difference was shown later to be noradrenaline.

The production of catecholamines is controlled by a series of enzymes (figure 5·1). To go at this point ahead of schedule, a condition known as phenylketonuria sometimes occurs. In this inborn error of metabolism, phenylalanine cannot, owing to the absence of the necessary enzyme, be converted into tyrosine. In consequence it accumulates in the body, and the child, for a reason that is not yet clear, is mentally defective. For a reason that is obvious from the figure, the child has a deficiency of adrenaline and noradrenaline. Moreover, it is from the stage of dopa that melanin is formed. Melanin is the brown substance in the skin and the child is therefore unpigmented. Dopamine, the next stage in the ultimate conversion of phenylalanine into noradrenaline and adrenaline, may have some bearing in its own right on the regulation of blood pressure (see chapter 13) and may be concerned also in some mental disorders (see chapter 12).

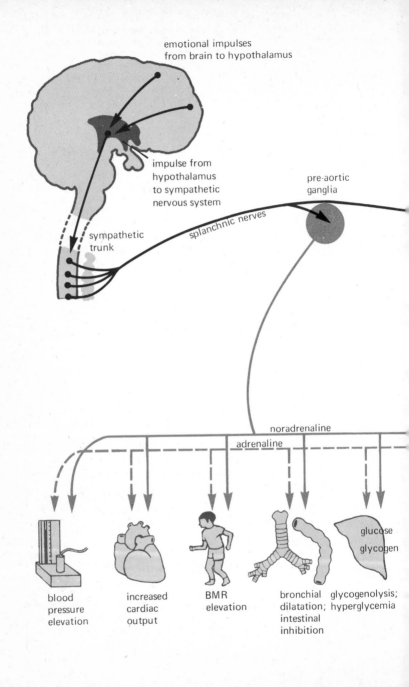

emotional impulses
from brain to hypothalamus

impulse from
hypothalamus
to sympathetic
nervous system

pre-aortic
ganglia

sympathetic
trunk

splanchnic nerves

noradrenaline

adrenaline

blood
pressure
elevation

increased
cardiac
output

BMR
elevation

bronchial
dilatation;
intestinal
inhibition

glycogenolysis;
hyperglycemia

glucose

glycogen

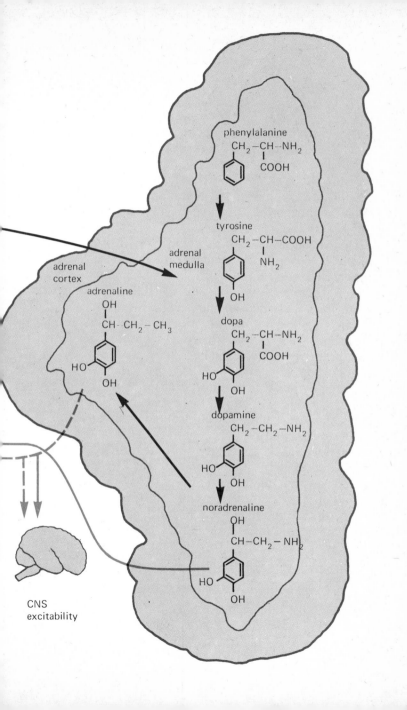

It has been mentioned that the catecholamines, of which adrenaline, noradrenaline and dopamine are found in the body, have different actions. Noradrenaline stimulates smooth muscle, whereas adrenaline may stimulate or inhibit according to circumstances. Noradrenaline has only a weak action in relaxing the bronchial muscles, but adrenaline has a strong one and is therefore of more use in asthma (see chapter 16). However, a synthetic derivative of noradrenaline known as N-isopropyl noradrenaline or isoprenaline is nine times as active in this respect as adrenaline. Dopamine is far weaker. On the blood pressure the difference in action of adrenaline and noradrenaline is still more pronounced. The former raises the systolic (the 'stroke' blood pressure), lowers the diastolic, (the 'between stroke' pressure) and leaves the mean pressure unaffected. The latter raises both systolic and diastolic pressures and therefore raises the mean pressure. Although by direct action noradrenaline quickens the heart, the raised blood pressure causes a reflex slowing which overcomes this quickening effect. Isoprenaline causes a fall in blood pressure and a quickening of the heart.

There are many apparent contradictions in the action of adrenaline. For instance, it contracts the uterus of the rabbit and relaxes that of the cat. Ahlquist has explained this by postulating two kinds of receptors on which it can act, α and β receptors. Adrenaline acts on both, whereas the action of noradrenaline is almost purely on α receptors. Typical α effects are contraction of smooth muscle in the vessels of the skin, mucous membranes and kidneys, a rise in blood pressure and slowing of the heart. Typical β effects are relaxation of smooth muscle, dilatation of blood vessels in muscle, and increased pulse rate and force of contraction of the heart.

For the lay reader the story of the adrenal medullary

hormones must seem somewhat confusing, but it can be simplified. There are two important hormones, chemically very closely related, adrenaline and noradrenaline, some of the actions of which are similar and some dissimilar. They act on the various organs in ways the dissimilarity of which depends partly on their different chemical constitution and partly because of differences within the organs themselves, some of which contain α receptors, which respond to adrenaline and noradrenaline in one way, and some β receptors which respond in another way. The whole story has not yet been unravelled.

6 The thyroid gland

The thyroid gland lies in the front of the neck. Its situation is well known to most people because of the set of conditions in which it becomes enlarged into a visible goitre. It produces three hormones, thyroxine, triiodothyronine, and calcitonin, the last only recently discovered. For reasons of convenience calcitonin will be described in the next chapter.

The role of iodine

Goitres were known from a very early time. They are referred to in the *Atharva Veda*, a Hindu religious work of 1500 BC or earlier, and in the *Ayurveda* of Sushruta of about 1400 BC. Even earlier Chinese physicians were treating the disease with burnt sponge and seaweed, both rich in iodine. Dwarfs, some of them probably cretins, appear in the folklore of many countries. Julius Caesar noticed that the Gauls had big necks. In his day, court dwarfs from the Alps were not employed – they were too stupid to be funny. Juvenal and Pliny both recognised the prevalence of goitres in alpine regions. Shakespeare, in *The Tempest*, asked: 'Who would believe that there were mountaineers dew-lapped like bulls, whose throats had hanging at them wallets of flesh?' The word 'mountaineer' has changed its meaning since and no one would ask this question of members of the Alpine Club.

That goitres might be related to diet was suggested by the great traveller Marco Polo in the thirteenth century. He described goitres in Yarkand and ascribed them to the water the people drank. Cold water was blamed for centuries, probably because snow water was drunk in alpine regions. Hard water was also blamed, a better guess. Michelangelo wrote: 'I've grown a goitre while living in this den [the Sistine Chapel!] as cast from stagnant streams in Lombardy.' The view that infected water is responsible was revived by McCarrison only thirty years ago. Nevertheless, gradually over the centuries, the view that iodine deficiency, though not recognised as such, was responsible for some goitres gradually gathered strength. Suddenly in the early nineteenth century the knowledge so slowly gathered fell into place like the pieces of a jig-saw. In 1812 Courtois accidentally discovered a lovely violet substance in his gun-powder vats. It was recognised as a new element by Gay-Lussac and named iodine. Numerous investigators soon recognised that the effects of various ancient remedies were due to its presence. It was first used knowingly in the treatment of goitre by the Englishman Prout in 1816, and Coindret soon established its value. As early as 1833 Boussingault recommended iodised salt as a preventative measure.

That iodine must have been remarkably effective, given in ancient times as seaweed or in modern times as the element or its salts, seems undoubted. Otherwise it could not have survived for at least 4,000 years. Yet today it is used only as a prophylactic or in preparation for surgical operation. The first function is of enormous importance. The first experiment on a large scale was carried out by Marine and Kimball among schoolgirls in Akron in 1917. Iodination of salt was introduced into Switzerland soon afterwards and resulted in the proportion of goitrous school children being reduced from 90% to 28%. Only medically backward nations in which goitre is a problem, among which Britain, despite many expert recommendations, must be numbered, have failed to introduce into the salt on sale in the shops the minute amount of iodine necessary to eliminate this type of goitre.

As a cure, as opposed to a preventative, iodine has in

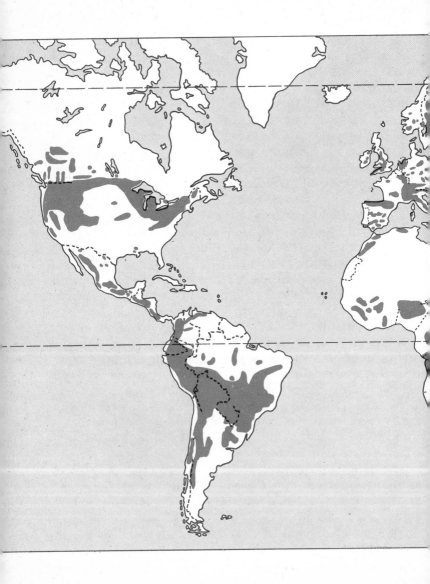

6·2 The structural formulae of the thyroid hormones and their precursors.

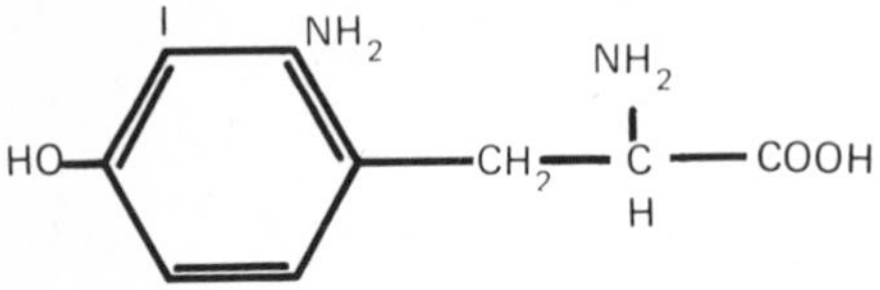

monoiodotyrosine (MIT

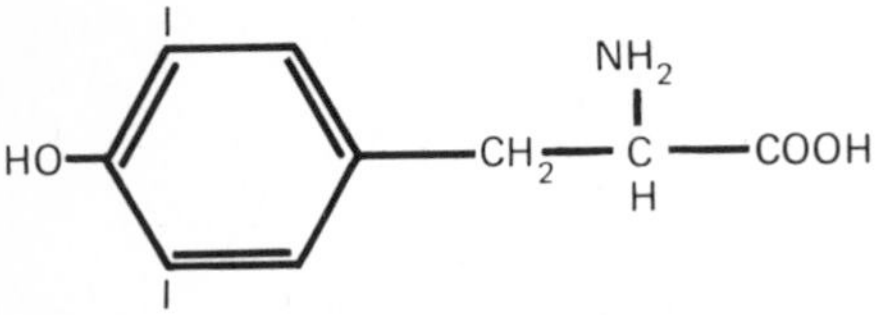

diiodotyrosine (DIT

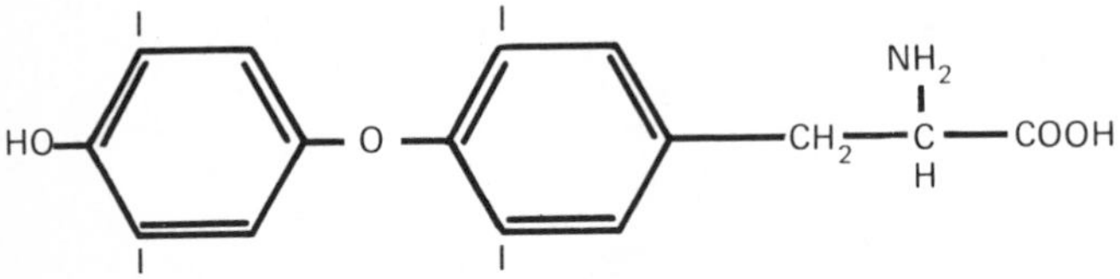

thyroxin

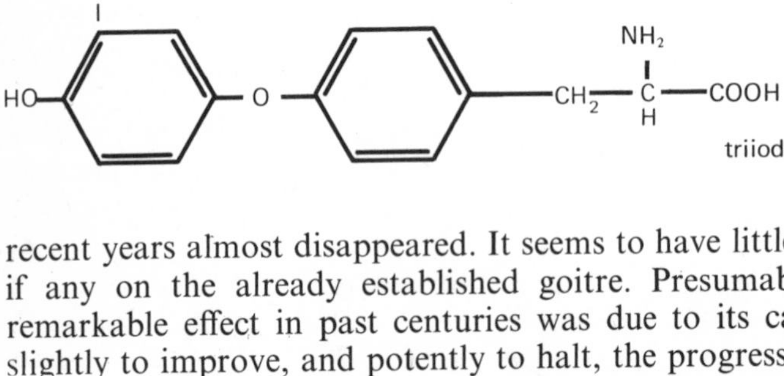

triiodothyronir

recent years almost disappeared. It seems to have little effect if any on the already established goitre. Presumably the remarkable effect in past centuries was due to its capacity slightly to improve, and potently to halt, the progress of the commonest type of goitre, that caused by iodine deficiency. The dramatic effects in this type presumably masked its failure to improve less common types.

Its use in the excessively active thyroid of Graves' disease has also had its day. Administered to a patient with thyrotoxicosis, it temporarily reduces the activity of the gland and it had an important use in the days before the discovery of the antithyroid drugs in tiding over to recovery the transient cases and in preparing others for operation. In the first it has been supplanted, though it still has an important use in making the thyroid of Graves' disease more amenable to surgery. As a cure for the established goitre it has lost its place.

The thyroid hormones

The production of thyroxine is better understood than that of any other hormone. The rate of its production is governed in health by the thyrotrophic hormone of the anterior pituitary gland. The raw material is iodine, which however administered, by injection, by mouth, or even through the skin, makes its way to the thyroid in the form of iodide, the rate at which it does so depending on the avidity of the gland. The avidity depends partly on the strength of pituitary stimulation and partly on the amount of iodine already trapped within the thyroid.

The second stage is the oxidation of iodine to iodide and its incorporation into molecules of tyrosine to form mono-iodotyrosine. The third stage is the further iodination of monoiodotyrosine converting it into diiodotyrosine. The fourth stage is the coupling of two molecules of diiodotyrosine to form the finished product thyroxine, the main hormone of the thyroid. At the same time one molecule of monoiodotyrosine joins one of diiodotyrosine to form triiodothyronine, the secondary hormone of the gland.

Each step in this complicated process is governed by enzymes and blocks may occur at any point, often giving rise to clinical thyroid deficiency. The feedback mechanism already described causes an increase in the output by the pituitary of thyroid-stimulating hormone and often a goitre results. The increased stimulation may or may not produce full compensation. The various forms of thyroidal deficiency shown in figure 6·3 are: 1. Iodide transport defect; 2. Iodide organification defect, sometimes associated with deafness, when it is called Pendred's syndrome, and sometimes complete, as in cretinism; 3. Thyroglobulin synthesis defect; 4. Dehalogenase defect, in which the patient cannot recover the iodine set free when the thyroid hormones are formed from mono- and diiodotyrosine but drains it away disastrously in the urine; 5. The coupling defect, in which the iodotyrosines do not join to form thyroxine and triiodothyronine; 6. A failure of the cells of the body as a whole to respond to the finished hormones. Another abnormality is an intrinsic failure of the thyroid cells to form thyroglobulin, a disease described in both men and sheep. In other cases abnormal products are produced. These diseases may be familial: as Stanbury, who has done so much to clarify the mystery of thyroid deficiency, has pointed out, the thyroid is not an essential organ. Life can continue and the reproductive capacity of the individual is not necessarily impaired. The various enzyme deficiencies may be passed on to future generations.

These chemical reactions occur within the molecules of thyroglobulin contained in the vesicles of the gland. It is there that most of the iodine in whatever form is stored. In ordinary circumstances little thyroglobulin is secreted into the blood. It must first be hydrolysed by an enzyme, protease, by means of which thyroxine and triiodothyronine are freed. Their smaller molecules can escape into the blood stream.

The factors which regulate this course of events are some-

6·3 The iodine cycle.

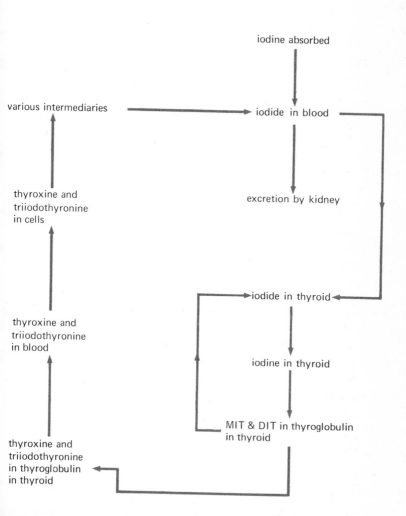

what complex. The relationship between the pituitary and the thyroid has already been mentioned briefly and the servo-mechanism described. Thyrotrophin increases thyroid activity by accelerating the uptake of iodide, but it stimulates also synthesis within the gland; that is the formation of iodotyrosines and their coupling into thyroxine.

Dietary factors are of great importance, our understanding of these having been helped greatly by the study of goitre occurring endemically in many parts of the world. The lack of the raw material iodine naturally causes a lack of the finished product. In consequence the output of thyrotrophin from the pituitary is increased in a vain effort to improve the efficiency of the thyroid. Unfortunately this can result in a quantitative change only and the gland increases in size, sometimes to an enormous degree, with little or no qualitative improvement.

Apart from this negative effect, the constituents of the diet may have a positive one. Rabbits fed exclusively on cabbage develop goitres, and other vegetables, notably rape, mustard, soya bean, ground nuts and turnips have been incriminated. In Tasmania and Australia the excessive ingestion of the brassica chou-moellia by cows has led to goitre in children drinking their milk. In several plants the actual 'goitrogens' have been found. These are sometimes cyanides, sometimes derivatives of thiocyanate, and they produce their effects by an interference, like that of the drugs soon to be mentioned, in the synthesis of thyroxine.

The first hint that drugs could affect the synthesis of thyroid hormone was given by the accidental appearance of goitres in patients treated for hypertension with thiocyanate. This effect could be reversed by iodide, from which it could be argued that the action of thiocyanate was to reduce the uptake of iodine by the thyroid. Thus alerted, research workers soon found other 'goitrogenic' drugs, notably thiourea, but their action was not reversed by iodide. It took place at a later stage of synthesis, and could be reversed only by thyroxine. From this work has arisen the discovery of a whole range of antithyroid drugs of great importance in the treatment of hyperthyroidism.

Another important modifying factor in the production of thyroxine is temperature. It has been known for a long time that the thyroids of animals are affected by cold. The thyroids of farm animals in North America contain three times as much iodine in summer as in winter. In cold weather the thyroids of rats and birds enlarge and become more active. But there is an important difference between short and prolonged exposure. Short exposures stimulate the thyroid more than long ones. Probably short exposures stimulate the production of the hypothalamic thyrotrophin-releasing factor, whereas more severe or prolonged exposure causes stress and the production of corticotrophin, which lowers thyroid function. In human medicine the importance of this is seen every winter when hospitals often receive as emergencies old and lonely women who have been exposed to cold in unheated rooms. Sometimes they have unrecognised thyroid deficiency and have been unable to respond to the cold by an increased output of thyroid hormones. They need treatment not only with these but with adrenal steroids. Occasionally the situation has been exacerbated by the previous use of such drugs as reserpine, given perhaps for high blood pressure, which block the response of the thyroid to cold.

Stress is a word which requires definition. The dictionary gives many, of which perhaps the nearest to its medical meaning is 'a demand upon energy'. It is a potentially harmful attack upon the body, demanding action. The main effect of stress, as we have seen, is increased activity of the adrenal glands. The secretion of adrenaline is increased, but it is doubtful whether this is important from the thyroid point of view. That of hydrocortisone is also increased and this depresses thyroid function. A reduction of thyroid function has been found in a variety of conditions, including starvation, radiation sickness, burns, surgical and accidental trauma, emotional disturbance, and severe infections.

Action of the thyroid hormones

These then are some of the circumstances which regulate the secretion of thyroxine and triiodothyronine. The exact partition of their effects in ordinary life and our adjustments to their secretion are still unknown. It is known that the effects of thyroxine are slow in appearing and slow in disappearing, whereas those of triiodothyronine are rapid in onset and rapid in offset. The effects of the former begin to be manifest in forty-eight hours, reach a zenith in two weeks, and can still be detected up to six weeks. Those of the latter appear in a few hours and disappear within a week or two. At one time the plausible hypothesis was advanced that in fact thyroxine had no physiological effect *per se* and that the delay and prolongation of its action were due to the fact that before it can do anything at all it must be slowly converted into triiodothyronine. It was an attractive idea, but it has not withstood the test of time. We do not know why these two hormones exist, nor what parts they play in the activity of thyroid hormone as a whole. However this may be, thyroxine represents the major thyroid hormone in circulation. Mono-

and diiodotyrosine are found in abnormal conditions only.

But there are complications still to be considered. Thyroxine and triiodothyronine do not circulate as pure substances only. They are largely bound in the circulation to proteins known as thyroxine-binding proteins or TBP. The physiological action of thyroxine appears to depend on the small quantities which are free and unbound to proteins. Thus the TBP is greatly increased in pregnancy, but the physiological effects expected of thyroxine are not increased. Triiodothyronine is not so readily bound to protein as thyroxine. In consequence it enters more easily and more rapidly into the cells.

Metabolic effects The physiological actions of the thyroid hormones are now well understood. Their fundamental activity is on the rate of cellular oxidation. There is a linear relationship between the circulating thyroid hormones and the basal metabolic rate (BMR), the rate at which oxygen is consumed in the subject completely at rest. Unfortunately in the human patient the attainment of absolute rest is impossible and in consequence the measurement of the BMR is a poor clinical criterion. Moreover, too little is still known about total metabolic activity throughout the resting night and the working day. The BMR is not necessarily a measure of this and in humans it is so subject to environmental considerations and emotional state that it is now rarely used as the simple test it was once thought to be of a patient's thyroid activity. Nevertheless, there is no doubt that the secretion of thyroid hormones exercises an important effect in regulating the internal temperature and thus in maintaining the constancy of the internal environment.

Maturation effects The second most obvious effect of thyroid hormones, most evident in animals, is on growth and maturation. This activity is probably quite independent of their effect on the rate of expenditure of energy, for other substances that raise the metabolic rate do not influence growth. Moreover excessive doses of thyroid hormone inhibit growth by inducing excessive catabolism but they still stimulate maturation. The exact way in which thyroid hormone stimulates growth is unknown, but it is probable that it does so by acting in partnership with the growth hormone of the anterior pituitary.

In all animals so far examined many tissues are subject to this influence. When there is a deficiency of thyroid hormone, general growth is retarded, skin and hair in mammals and feathers in birds are improperly formed, infantile bone structure persists, sexual development fails, teeth are deformed and their eruption is delayed. All these abnormalities are corrected when thyroid hormone is administered.

But perhaps the most dramatic effects may be seen in the metamorphosis of some lower vertebrates. In the absence of the thyroid gland, tadpoles continue to grow and may reach gigantic size, but they do not change into frogs. Conversely, the axolotl, which in nature retains for life the appearance of a gigantic tadpole, responds to thyroid hormone by developing limbs. This is the only known example of the creation by artificial means of what is essentially a new man-made animal.

Effects on the nervous system Thyroid hormone is necessary for the development of the brain in early life, and a deficiency then may be irreparable. Without it the constituent neurones are unable to absorb from the blood the nutrients necessary for the synthesis of protein, the enzyme necessary for the process being absent. At any age there is a direct relationship between the levels of thyroid activity and the use of oxygen in the brain. This matter and the profound relationship between thyroid activity and the autonomic nervous system will be considered more fully in a later chapter. The cretin is an example of the irreparability of the effects of thyroid deficiency in early life.

Effects on lactation The effects of thyroid hormone on the production of milk has, of course, great economic interest. Deficiency lowers the production of milk. Feeding dried thyroid gland to cows increases not only the amount of milk produced but its content of fat. Similar results follow the administration of artificial iodinated proteins which are cheaper but need biological standardisation. Although the question has not been settled finally, it is likely that the effect of thyroid hormone on lactation is a reflection of its capacity to increase the blood supply of the breasts.

Other physiological effects of thyroid hormone Thyroid hormone has what is known as a diuretic effect, by which is meant an increase in the output of urine. When it is deficient water and salt accumulate in some of the tissues of the body, notably outside the cells. The mechanism of this action is still unsettled. It has an important effect on protein metabolism, having in normal and thyrotoxic subjects a catabolic effect and in hypothyroid ones an anabolic one. This apparent contradiction may be due to the balancing effect of other hormones, for the male sex hormones can overcome the former effect. A fact that has aroused great interest because of its possible importance in cardiac disease is the lowering effect of thyroid hormones on the level of cholesterol and other fats in the blood. It is probable that thyroid hormones accelerate the rate of synthesis of cholesterol in the liver as well as their breakdown. In health there is a fine balance, but an underactive thyroid favours increased synthesis and an overactive one increased breakdown. The effects of thyroid hormone on the cardiovascular system will be described in chapter 13.

The effect of the thyroid on calcium metabolism has been realised for many years. It was known, for instance, that in overactivity of the thyroid, the calcium excretion is increased, maybe to eight times the normal amount, the increase being evident both in urine and faeces. This increase may be produced by the administration of thyroxine. Many patients with hyperthyroidism show osteoporosis, a thinning of the bones. The activity of thyroxine is not due to increased metabolism, for in some cases the increase in calcium excretion is out of proportion to the rise in metabolic rate. In, for instance, fevers and leukaemia there is a great increase in metabolism without any change in calcium excretion. Nor is it likely that thyroxine exerts its effect by way of the parathyroid glands (chapter 7) for there is usually no alteration in the blood level of calcium in hyperthyroidism. The effect of thyroxine may be upon the renal threshold for calcium. In recent years the discovery of calcitonin has partly clarified our ideas.

Too much and too little

The disease caused by too much thyroid secretion was first described by Caleb Parry in 1786, but the first good description was by Robert Graves of Dublin in 1835. The disease is still known in the English-speaking countries as Graves'

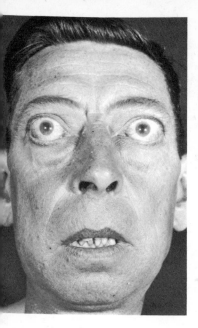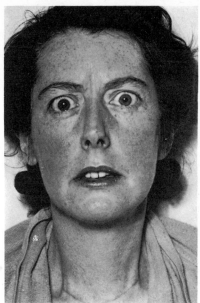

disease. Independently Basedow described it in 1890, and in many continental countries it is still known as Basedow's disease. The reader of this chapter can already guess the features of Graves' disease. Increased cellular metabolism throughout the body leads to a general acceleration of all bodily and mental processes. The patient in consequence becomes nervous and excitable and (unless as sometimes happens the appetite is enormously increased) loses weight. Movements are quick and restless. The overactivity of the sympathetic nervous system causes the heart to beat unduly fast; the skin is hot and flushed and sweating is increased; the eyes stare. The third component of the syndrome, protrusion of the eyes, known as exophthalmos, is still unexplained: it does not always occur. There are many other less obvious effects of excessive thyroid secretion, some of which will be mentioned in later chapters, but it should be remembered that almost any sign or symptom may be absent in an individual patient.

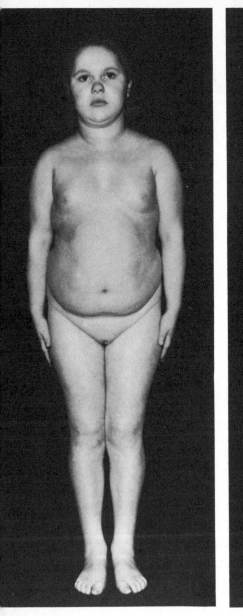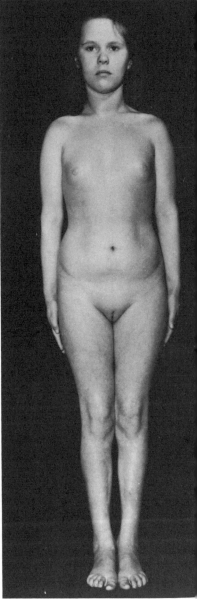

6·6 Infantile thyroid deficiency. Treatment
for only one year produced an increase in height
of $2\frac{1}{2}$ inches, the disappearance of obesity,
a remarkable change in the facial contours
and the first signs of puberty. The girl's
intelligence, previously deficient, became normal.

79

The cause of excessive thyroid secretion, resulting in Graves' disease, is only now becoming clear. The work of Adams and others has shown that it is due to a substance, a globulin, circulating in the blood. It is known as the long-acting thyroid stimulator or LATS for short. It seems to be a substance produced by what is known as an autoimmune reaction, a process in which the body becomes sensitive to something within itself. There are many diseases thought to have a somewhat similar origin, including some cases of Addison's disease, as we have already seen, another thyroid disorder called Hashimoto's disease, many cases of thyroid deficiency as opposed to excess, rheumatoid arthritis, and pernicious anaemia.

Deficiency of the thyroid produces in general the opposite effects. The mind and body work more slowly, the skin is cold, and sweating is deficient. The weight tends to increase: the heart beats slowly: water is often retained in the tissues. An additional mysterious fact is the accumulation in the tissues of a substance called mucopolysaccharide (see chapter 18), and curiously enough there may be a protrusion of the eyes like that in the opposite condition of the thyroid. Of thyroid deficiency, or myxoedema, it is even more true than of thyroid excess that most of the symptoms and signs may be absent, only one part of the body bearing obviously the brunt of the disease. Cretinism, a condition in which thyroid deficiency is present before birth, was described by Paracelsus in Salzburg in the sixteenth century but it was only in the nineteenth century that the researches of Gull, the son of a poor Essex boatman who became a baronet and a royal physician, of Ord, Schiff, Horsley and others established the fact that cretinism in children and myxoedema in adults are due to thyroid deficiency. The existence of an internal secretion

6·7 Below left Adult myxoedema. Note the highly coloured cheek bones, the obesity, and the swelling of the eyelids (producing a 'pig-like' look).

6·8 Below right Cretinism. The thyroid has been deficient from early foetal life. The patient is an idiot. Note especially the depression of the bridge of the nose and the vacant expression.

 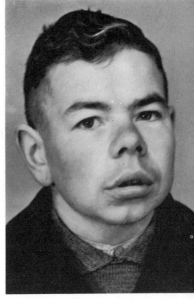

of the thyroid was first realised by Wilkinson King of Guy's Hospital in London in 1836. The first man to use thyroid extract in the treatment of thyroid deficiency was Murray in 1891.

7 The thyroid-parathyroid partnership

The thyroid has, as part of its function, and the parathyroid as the whole of its function, the regulation of calcium metabolism, the thyroid hormone concerned being calcitonin and the parathyroid hormone parathormone.

Calcium is of the utmost importance from many points of view. In the first place it is, in the form of calcium phosphate, the hard part of bone. Ninety-nine per cent of the body's calcium is contained there. But bone is not just a scaffold. It is a very active tissue that is continuously remodelled, bone destruction always, in health, being balanced by bone formation. It is the reservoir for calcium for use elsewhere. From the bones calcium is drawn in order to preserve normal neuromuscular activity, to meet the needs of the growing foetus during pregnancy and of the breasts during lactation. It is necessary in blood coagulation. It affects the contractility of all muscle, including that of the heart, and the transmission of impulses at the junctions between nerves and between nerves and muscles; the presence of calcium reduces their irritability. These miscellaneous activities are paramount. If the supply of calcium is insufficient, it is drawn from bone, sometimes, as in rickets, to its detriment. The two-way traffic between bone and blood is controlled by parathormone, the hormone of the parathyroid gland, and by calcitonin, derived chiefly from the C cells or parafollicular cells of the thyroid, thymus and parathyroid. Parathormone withdraws calcium from bone; calcitonin inhibits the withdrawal.

Parathormone

The metabolism of calcium cannot be discussed apart from that of phosphorus, a constituent of every cell. In most circumstances a rise in plasma phosphorus leads to a reduction

7·1 Calcium metabolism.

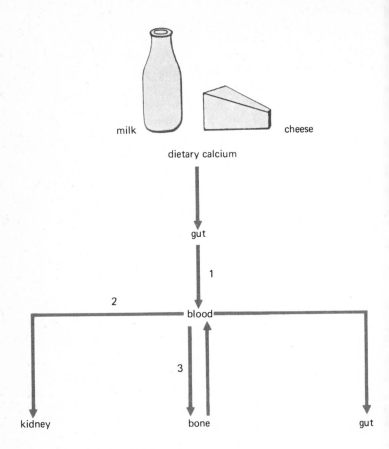

1 Absorption decreased in gut by phosphate, potassium, magnesium, wheat (phytate), malabsorption syndrome.

Absorption increased by need, vitamin D, parathormone, lactose.

2 Increased by thyroxine and parathormone.

3 Increased by parathormone, decreased by calcitonin.

in plasma calcium. Parathormone decreases the amount of phosphorus reabsorbed by the tubules of the kidneys. Thus the amount of phosphorus in the urine rises, that in the blood falls, and in consequence the calcium in the blood rises.

The parathyroid hormone has yet another effect: it increases the absorption of calcium from the gut. This is not always easy. The hormone is hindered by the presence of potassium, magnesium and phosphate, but is assisted by lactose and vitamin D. Its elimination from the body is chiefly through the lining mucous membrane of the intestine, only a little in the urine. The colon usually contains a lot of calcium consisting of unabsorbed residue and a proportion that has been re-excreted.

We see then that parathormone raises the level of calcium in the blood in three ways. It withdraws calcium from the bones, it increases the output of phosphorus by the kidneys, and it aids absorption from the gut.

Too much and too little Too much parathormone, due usually to a tumour of one of the parathyroid glands, has a devastating effect. It may show itself in the bones or the kidneys. Too much calcium is withdrawn from the bones, which become weak and liable to bend or break. Owing to the increase in calcium passing through the kidneys stones are deposited there and infection often follows. In general the sufferer is unduly tired, loses appetite and weight and suffers from nausea, vomiting, and other digestive disorders. Calcium may be deposited in the cornea of the eyes and elsewhere.

When there is too little parathormone, most commonly because the parathyroids have been accidentally removed during an operation on the thyroid, the main brunt falls upon the nervous system. Unrestrained by calcium it becomes over-irritable. Tetany, a violent form of cramp, is the most dramatic occurrence, but lesser evils such as 'pins and needles' are common. Epilepsy may occur. Mental effects are frequent, especially anxiety and listlessness. True psychosis, if the cause goes unrecognised, may lead to incarceration in a mental hospital.

Calcitonin

This new hormone, discovered by Copp as recently as 1962, has as its sole known function the inhibition of the withdrawal of calcium from bone, balancing in this respect the effects of parathormone. It was thought at first that it was secreted only by the parathyroids, but MacIntyre and his colleagues in London have shown that it is in fact produced also by special cells of the thyroid, the C cells or parafollicular cells, and to a lesser extent by similar cells in the thymus gland and the parathyroids. These cells have emigrated from organs called the ultimobranchial bodies, well known in birds and fish and long suspected of having an endocrine function.

Too much and too little The clinical significance of calcitonin has still to be explored. It might be useful in lowering the excessive load of calcium in the blood of some patients with malignant disease, often accompanied by most distressing nausea. It may possibly prove of value in osteoporosis, the still mysterious thinning of bone in many old people. It may be that the difficulty we have in maintaining the correct level of calcium in the blood of patients whose thyroid and parathyroids have been removed is due to an absence of the balancing action of calcitonin. The hormone has now been synthesised and it seems likely that much more will soon be known.

8 The pancreas

Like so many other glands the pancreas has a double function. By means of a duct it conveys digestive juice to the intestine, its exocrine function. But it contains within it a specialised group of cells, the islets of Langerhans, that have an endocrine function, the secretion of insulin, a protein, and glucagon, hormones intimately concerned with the regulation of the blood sugar. The intermittent demands for energy for physical and metabolic work are met by glucose. This is stored in the cells in the form of glycogen. For the transfer of glucose from the blood to the cell interior, insulin is necessary. Once there, a long chain of enzyme actions converts it into glycogen. Another chain is responsible for its return journey to glucose. Inherited deficiencies of any of the numerous enzymes involved are responsible for breakdowns at various points and consequent diseases.

Insulin

When carbohydrate, sugar or starch is eaten by a healthy person, it is converted by the digestive juices into the monosaccharides, glucose, laevulose and galactose, of which glucose is by far the most important. These are absorbed and carried to the liver, where, in all probability, the laevulose and galactose are ultimately converted into glucose. Some of the glucose passes thence directly into the systemic circulation, but much of it is converted into glycogen and stored. The glucose which passes into the circulation is partly used in the production of energy, and partly stored as glycogen, especially in the muscles, any excess being converted rapidly into fat. Normally no appreciable glucose is excreted by the kidneys, but if for any reason the amount in the bloodstream exceeds the threshold value (which in the majority of people is approximately 180 mg per 100 ml), it appears in the urine. The liver glycogen is again broken down into glucose when the blood sugar falls.

The level of glucose in the blood stream is regulated by:

1 *Ingestion.* The main source of glucose is ingested carbohydrate. Of other substances which may be stored as glycogen and may therefore indirectly raise the blood sugar, the most important is protein.

2 *Absorption.* In some conditions of deficient intestinal efficiency, the blood sugar is low.

3 *Gluconeogenesis.* The production of glucose from other foods.

4 *Glycogenesis.* The conversion of glucose into glycogen. Insulin is necessary for efficient glycogenesis.

5 *Glycogenolysis*, that is, the conversion of glycogen into glucose. This process occurs in response to a low blood sugar and is at any rate partly under the control of the sympathetic nervous system. Rapid mobilisation of liver glycogen follows injection of adrenaline, which itself is excreted in increased quantity when the blood sugar is low, and under the influence of emotion. Glycosuria, sugar in the urine, has been observed in students awaiting a *viva voce* examination. Rapid glycogenolysis occurs also after injection of pitressin or thyroxine, in asphyxia and in anaesthesia.

6 *Utilisation.* The traditional explanation of diabetes assumed that the sole, or at least the main, defect was a failure of the tissues properly to use glucose in the absence of a proper supply of insulin. It is, indeed, true that at any given blood-sugar level the diabetic animal uses less sugar than does the normal animal, but this fact is of little significance because the diabetic person has a higher blood-sugar level, enabling him to use sugar as well as does the healthy person.

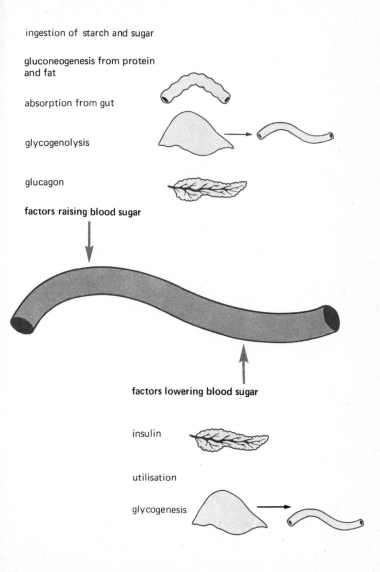

ingestion of starch and sugar

gluconeogenesis from protein
and fat

absorption from gut

glycogenolysis

glucagon

factors raising blood sugar

factors lowering blood sugar

insulin

utilisation

glycogenesis

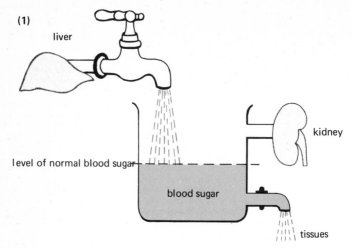

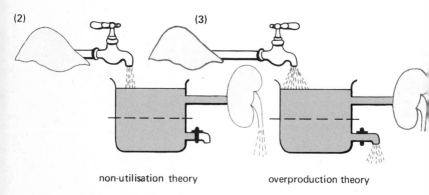

The central organ in the regulation of the blood-sugar level is the liver, the storehouse of sugar from whatever source it may be derived. The activities of the various hormones of the anterior pituitary, the adrenal cortex, the thyroid and the pancreas may be examined from three points of view: 1. Their action upon the uptake and output of sugar by the liver;

2. Their action in augmenting or retarding the various stages in the metabolism of carbohydrates; 3. Their influence on the mobilisation of proteins and fats.

The theory that diabetes is due to a failure of the tissues to use glucose received its death-blow when it was found that removal of the liver results in a low blood sugar, whether or not the pancreas has previously been removed. If the high blood sugar of diabetes is not due to a failure to use glucose it must necessarily be due to overproduction. The two contrasting theories are well illustrated by Soskin's diagram.

In (1) the liver, represented by the tap above the tank, is pouring into the blood just as much sugar as the tissues, represented by the lowest tap, are drawing off. (2) shows the non-utilisation theory. The tissues cannot use sugar, so the lowest tap is closed and the excess of sugar above the proper level is 'wasted' into the urine. The removal of the liver should cause a drop in the level to the renal threshold but not below. This, as we have seen, is not the case. (3) represents the overproduction theory. The lowest tap remains open but, because the upper tap pours in an excessive amount, an overflow occurs. If the tap is turned off by removal of the liver, the sugar continues to be used and the blood sugar falls.

It has been found that the use of sugar by the tissues is at most levels proportional to the level of the blood sugar, whether or not the experimental animal has been rendered diabetic. Though at any given blood-sugar level the diabetic animal uses slightly less sugar, the upper limit at which a further increase in utilisation ceases, about 450 mg per 100 ml, is the same in both normal and diabetic animals. In fact though insulin may make slightly easier the utilisation of sugar by the tissues, this utilisation does occur even in the diabetic animal.

However obscure the mechanism may be we have reached a point at which we may say that the level of sugar in the blood is kept in balance by insulin which lowers it when it is too high, and the pituitary, adrenal cortex and thyroid which raise it when it is too low. To this regulation only one organ, the liver, is absolutely necessary. In health the main regulation of the blood sugar is by insulin, to which the liver constantly responds by increasing or decreasing its output of glucose from the glycogen in its stores. In this process the endocrines 'set the temperature of the furnace'. In diabetes mellitus the 'temperature' is set too high: in the presence of a tumour of the islets of Langerhans it is set too low. Overactivity of the adrenal cortex sets it too high, underactivity too low. Exactly how this regulation is brought about is still unknown in detail. In general terms we are viewing the action of the various hormones on the various enzymes involved.

There are a large number of questions about insulin still to be answered. We do not yet know in what form it circulates in the blood, whether free or combined with some other protein. We are still rather vague about the manner in which the level of insulin varies in diabetes mellitus. Controversy is still going on about the presence in the blood of insulin antagonists. Nevertheless great progress has been made in the determination of the structure of insulin. In the ox it consists of two chains of amino acids, wrapped round each other, the so-called A chain having twenty-one amino acids and the B chain thirty. There are however considerable species differences between the insulin of one animal and another, and the exact structure of human insulin is still unknown. These differences produce a problem in the treatment of diabetes because the patient treated with insulin derived from an animal may occasionally treat it as a foreign protein and become allergic to it. In very recent years substances with the activity of insulin have been synthesised and big practical advances seem just round the corner.

Insulin is produced only by the islets of Langerhans, where it is stored in the so-called β cells, the granules of which are released in response to sugar, corticotrophin, glucagon, and certain drugs used in the treatment of diabetes. Conversely, the release of insulin is decreased by various substances, of which adrenaline is the most important, and when the concentration of calcium and potassium is low. The level of insulin in the blood is also affected by diet, restriction of carbohydrate increasing it and complete starvation decreasing it.

When first insulin was discovered it was not unnaturally thought that diabetes mellitus was due simply to the failure of the pancreas to produce it in sufficient quantity, so that glucose accumulated in the blood and, instead of being used by the tissues of the body, was wasted in the urine. There would thus be an excess of glucose in blood and urine and a deficiency in the cells, a concept which does indeed explain most of the symptoms of the disease, and is still considered to be largely true in very severe cases, and partially true in many milder ones. However in the obese mildly diabetic person, most commonly when the disease has appeared in middle age, the amount of insulin secreted is often greater than normal, and it is supposed that their illness is due to the presence of antagonists to insulin.

It is well-known that diabetes is a familial disease. It has been shown that the healthy relatives of known diabetics often have a low level of insulin in their blood. In such families, the islets of Langerhans may fail to respond normally to the stimulus of a high level of glucose in the blood.

Another suggested explanation is that such families inherit as a Mendelian dominant an excessive amount of an antagonist to insulin.

Glucagon

The presence of a second hormone with an action on the blood sugar opposite to that of insulin was detected within a year of Banting and Best's great discovery of insulin, but little advance in our knowledge of the second hormone took place until recent years. It seems to have been overshadowed by its sister, rendered glamorous by her life-saving effects on diabetics, until 1922 condemned to die of their disease.

Like insulin glucagon is a protein. In the pig it consists of a single chain of twenty-nine amino acids. It is produced by the α cells of the pancreas, but not exclusively. It, or anyway a very similar substance, has been extracted from the stomach and intestines.

The liver is generally thought to be the most important field of its activity. It increases glycogenolysis and gluconeogenesis. It may also affect fat metabolism within the liver and in fat cells it has a lipolytic action, releasing free fatty acids and glycerol. A recent important discovery is that glucagon has a stimulating effect on the β cells of the islets of Langerhans, increasing the output of insulin directly and not merely because it raises the blood sugar. By some it is thought that this is indeed its primary physiological action, to stimulate the secretion of insulin in response to ingested glucose.

Glucagon has many other effects, some of which may be very important in human health and ill health. It stimulates the release of adrenaline and noradrenaline and indeed the rise in blood sugar produced by glucagon fails in animals from whom the adrenal medulla has been removed. It raises the level of potassium in the blood stream and reduces the contractions of the stomach and intestines and the acidity of the gastric juice.

The secretion of glucagon is controlled by several factors. The most important is a fall in the blood sugar. In starvation, the level in the blood may rise to three times the normal. It has been called the hormone of glucose need. Somewhat confusing therefore is the finding that the ingestion of a large dose of glucose induces a rise in the level of glucagon in the blood and with this an increase in the release of insulin. It would appear that a double mechanism is involved. In the first place a fall in the level of sugar in the blood induces an increased secretion of glucagon to correct this state: in the second place a load of sugar in the stomach induces an increased secretion in order to produce, in time to deal with it, an increased secretion of insulin.

In human patients a deficiency of glucagon has been postulated in infants with hypoglycaemia (McQuarrie's syndrome) and in young patients with diabetes mellitus who are excessively sensitive to insulin. An excess of glucagon has been suggested in mild adult-type diabetes and in a few patients with what seem to be tumours of the α cells of the pancreas. The whole question of the clinical significance of excess or deficiency of glucagon is still in doubt, but will probably be resolved rapidly now that glucagon has been synthesised.

9 The ovary

The ovaries have two functions, the production of ova and the secretion of the two hormones, oestradiol and progesterone. From birth they contain primitive ova which later develop and make their way to the uterus through the fallopian tubes to await fertilisation or disappointment. Originally there are about 400,000 primitive ova of which only a small proportion reach maturity. They lie inactive in the ovary through childhood. At puberty, in response to a signal of which nothing is known, the hypothalamus causes the anterior pituitary to discharge the gonadotrophic hormones already stored there. The girl, under the influence of oestradiol and progesterone, develops the outward form of the woman and at the same time under the same influences the uterus develops and after a short interval menstruation begins. The production of mature ova may occur then or a little later. Usually only one ovum is produced in each monthly or menstrual cycle. The two pituitary gonadotrophic hormones control the whole complicated process of ovulation and menstruation.

In the first half of the menstrual cycle the follicle stimulating hormone is in the ascendant. During this time several ovarian follicles, the envelopes in which the maturing ova lie, increase in size and some reach maturity. One ovum, occasionally two and rarely more, bursts from its follicle and enters the fallopian tube leading to the uterus. Meanwhile, again under the influence of the follicle stimulating hormone, which causes the secretion of oestradiol by the ovary, changes occur in the lining of the uterus, in preparation for the reception of the mature ovum. Immediately after ovulation the cells lining the now empty follicle begin to proliferate and to fill the follicle, forming a temporary endocrine gland called the corpus luteum. This temporary gland, now under the

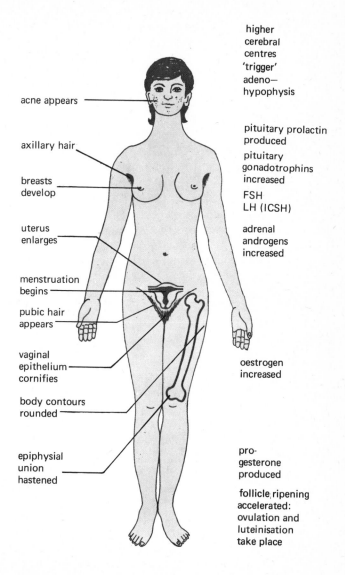

higher
cerebral
centres
'trigger'
adeno—
hypophysis

pituitary prolactin
produced

pituitary
gonadotrophins
increased

FSH
LH (ICSH)

adrenal
androgens
increased

oestrogen
increased

pro-
gesterone
produced

follicle ripening
accelerated:
ovulation and
luteinisation
take place

acne appears

axillary hair

breasts
develop

uterus
enlarges

menstruation
begins

pubic hair
appears

vaginal
epithelium
cornifies

body contours
rounded

epiphysial
union
hastened

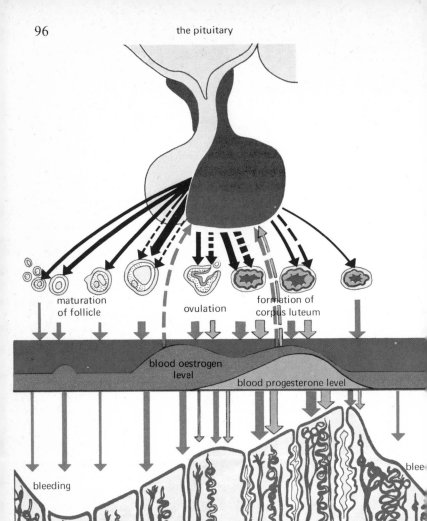

maturation
of follicle

ovulation

formation of
corpus luteum

blood oestrogen
level

blood progesterone level

bleeding

blee

0   days   14   days   28

proliferative phase   secretory phase

key

follicle stimulating hormone
luteinising hormone
oestrogen
progesterone

inhibition

influence of the luteal hormone of the pituitary, secretes progesterone. Progesterone changes the pattern of the lining of the uterus, completing its preparation for the reception of the ovum, acting in partnership with oestradiol which continues to be secreted. Without the concomitant action of oestradiol the changes typical of progestogenic activity do not occur. After about a fortnight of progestogenic action one of two things may happen. The ovum may have been fertilised by a spermatozoon and become embedded in the uterus, to continue to grow and mature for nine months, the correct pattern of the endometrium being maintained by a persistent corpus luteum. This continues to function under the influence of a hormone, produced by the embryo, which is identical with the pituitary luteinising hormone. At about three months the embryo, the placental part in particular, assumes complete control. If no fertilisation occurs, luteinising hormone is not produced, the corpus luteum degenerates, and the ovum is left loose in the uterus, from which it is discharged. The end of the secretion of both follicle stimulating and luteinising hormone by the pituitary causes a drop in the secretion of both ovarian hormones, and the lining of the uterus, the endometrium, is cast out at menstruation.

The changes in the endometrium at menstruation are caused by constriction of the arteries in its deeper parts. At intervals some of the arteries relax and rupture. Blood accumulates beneath the endometrium which is thus separated from the muscular wall of the uterus and shed. Then constriction of the arteries occurs and gradually the normal circulation is restored and regeneration of the endometrium occurs.

Menstruation can thus be regarded as a mechanism by which the endometrium is periodically prepared for pregnancy. It is essentially a passive process which can be reproduced in the absence of the ovaries by the administration of the ovarian hormones in the correct sequence. When both hormones are withdrawn a discharge of endometrium and blood occurs that is indistinguishable from normal menstruation. The same may be seen to occur even in the absence of ovulation, when the endometrium is maintained by oestradiol alone, though its pattern is very different from that seen when both hormones act upon it.

Though the outward signs and symptoms of puberty and menstruation are due to the general and local effects of the two ovarian hormones, they in their turn are controlled by the anterior pituitary, and here the servo-mechanism so often seen in the endocrine system also plays an important part. A high concentration of oestradiol inhibits the secretion of follicle-stimulating hormone and a high concentration of progesterone inhibits the secretion of luteinising hormone. Thus the high output of oestradiol at the time of ovulation reduces the secretion of the first but allows that of the second to continue. Towards the end of the second fortnight of the cycle the rising tide of progesterone stops the secretion of luteinising hormone. In consequence at the end of the cycle both gonadotrophins are at a low ebb, oestradiol and progesterone both fall and menstruation occurs.

The oestrogens

Strictly speaking, the word oestrogen denotes any substance that will cause cornification of the vagina of the adult mouse like that which occurs in natural oestrus or 'heat'. But the word has a much wider meaning. The ovary produces several oestrogens and of these the most important is oestra-

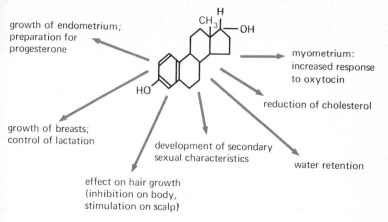

growth of endometrium; preparation for progesterone

myometrium: increased response to oxytocin

reduction of cholesterol

growth of breasts; control of lactation

development of secondary sexual characteristics

water retention

effect on hair growth (inhibition on body, stimulation on scalp)

diol. The different functions of the natural oestrogens are still not quite clear, and those of oestradiol may be taken as typical of the group. The elucidation of the functions of the oestrogens has been made more difficult by the fact that they are secreted not only by the ovary but by the placenta, the adrenal cortex and even by the testes. Only minute quantities are found in the organs that secrete them because they do not store their products but discharge them rapidly into the blood stream.

Like the other steroid hormones, the oestrogens of the ovary are derived from acetate by way of cholesterol and, confusingly, of testosterone. Neither the adrenal cortex nor the ovary itself is necessary for this manufacturing sequence, which is carried out by other tissues, especially, in pregnancy, by the placenta. It may even be effected by bacteria. Moreover, oestrogens are contained in several foods.

Oestradiol is responsible for the development of the female body at puberty. The uterus increases in size, the breasts develop and the whole body changes from that of a child into that of a woman. The endometrium, the lining of the uterus, develops in thickness. While the supply of oestradiol lasts,

9·4 Delayed puberty : before and after treatment with an oestrogen. The hips have broadened, the pubic hair has increased, the breasts have enlarged, the features have become more adult and menstruation has begun. Pigmentation of the nipples is likely in brunettes treated in this way.

the endometrium continues to thicken, but if it drops (as it does at the end of the menstrual cycle) the lining is cast away and menstruation ensues. The control by the pituitary of this cyclical process has already been described.

The more general actions of oestradiol are numerous. Perhaps the most obvious effect is on growth. In every mammal, including man, the male tends to be larger than the female. From an early age it checks growth perhaps by inhibiting the production of growth hormone by the pituitary. When it begins to be secreted in a larger amount at puberty, it stops altogether the growth of the long bones by producing bony union of the ends of the bones (the epiphyses) and their shafts (the metaphyses). Oestradiol also affects the amount and distribution of fat, the average female having more fat in her body than the male and having a tendency to lay it down in different places. It does not apparently inhibit the development of muscle, the relative muscular weakness of the woman being due not to more oestradiol but to less testosterone. It does, however, inhibit the growth of hair on the face, limbs and (apart from the pubes) the trunk, whereas it increases that on the scalp.

Oestradiol causes retention of water within the tissues. This is most obvious in the sexual skin of female monkeys, but even in women it occurs and is not confined to the vulva. There is in the normal woman a regular fluctuation in weight during the menstrual cycle, an increase occurring at the time of ovulation and just before menstruation, when the amount of oestradiol in the blood is greatest. But perhaps the general effect of oestradiol that has attracted most attention in recent years is the reduction of fatty substances in the blood, an effect which may be related, as we shall see in chapter 13, to the ever-present problem of coronary disease.

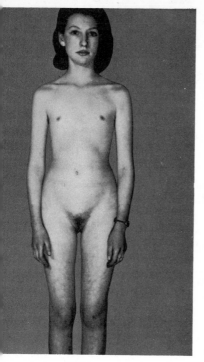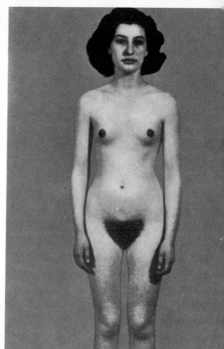

Progesterone

As we have seen, ovulation, occurring at about the middle of the normal menstrual cycle, initiates the formation of a corpus luteum in the ovary and the secretion of progesterone. This also is a steroid hormone, derived from cholesterol. It appears to have little action in developing the body as a whole, except the breasts. Its main activity is to cause the development of the endometrium, which develops mucous glands and is made ready for the reception of an ovum. A continuing supply of progesterone is necessary for the maintenance of an endometrium capable of maintaining the ovum. After three months, the responsibility for this supply is assumed by the placenta. If it fails, the endometrium decays and abortion occurs.

Progesterone decreases both the natural rhythmic contractions of the uterine muscle and its response to oxytocin, one of the hormones stored in the posterior pituitary gland. These effects are opposite to those of oestradiol and are important in maintaining the quiescence of the uterus during pregnancy. It may be concerned with the nutrition of the developing foetus. By its action on the pituitary it prevents ovulation during pregnancy.

Though in many of its activities progesterone is antagonistic to oestradiol, in other spheres the two ovarian hormones act in partnership. Unless previously primed with oestradiol, the endometrium does not respond to progesterone. Oestradiol and progesterone act together in producing growth of the breasts in preparation for lactation.

Little is known about the more distant effects of progesterone, apart from the fact that in many respects it balances those of oestradiol. By analogy with other hormones we are justified in thinking that much has yet to be discovered.

Disorders of menstruation

These may arise at many levels in the endocrine hierarchy. It is probable that the commonest causes are psychological. A woman fearing the possibility of pregnancy after illicit intercourse commonly ceases to menstruate. Six per cent of the young women joining the WAAF in the second world war ceased to menstruate for many months. This is also a common occurrence in probationer nurses fresh from the protection of their homes, estimates varying from twenty-nine to fifty per cent. Sixty to seventy per cent of women confined in concentration camps ceased to have periods for months or even years. An absence of menstruation is invariable in the

CH₃
|
C = O

growth of breasts; partnership in lactation

CH₃

CH₃

O

relaxant effect on myometrium; reduces effect of oxytocin

anti-aldosterone effect

increased excretion of oestradiol

secretory changes in endometrium; maintenance of fertilised ovum

nervous disorder called anorexia nervosa, in which the patient embarks on a course of self-starvation. That in some at least of these patients the failure to menstruate is not the result of starvation is shown by the fact that it may precede loss of weight.

Menstrual disorders may also arise at the level of the anterior pituitary. In Simmonds' disease and Sheehan's disease, already mentioned in chapter 3, menstruation ceases. If the regular production of the gonadotrophic hormones is deranged, irregularity occurs because the ovary is no longer instructed in the regular production of oestradiol and progesterone. The regular production may break down because of disorder within the ovary itself. All the disorders of menstruation are now explicable by psychological, hypothalamic, pituitary or ovarian abnormalities and happily can almost always be treated along endocrine lines. The days of casual and often thoughtless removal of the uterus, common a generation ago, are happily no longer with us.

The menopause

The 'change of life' when menstrual periods cease is a time to dread for many women. This mistaken impression arises from the unfortunate female trait of discussing and magnifying minor symptoms over tea.

The climacteric, the period of diminishing ovarian activity, begins usually in the fourth decade of life. In many women, ovulation becomes less regular and in consequence the menstrual cycle comes to vary in length. The menstrual loss may be excessive or prolonged, a complication easily eliminated by treatment with a progestogen. The output of oestradiol by the ovary begins to vary, another cause of irregularity. Finally the ovary becomes completely irresponsive to pituitary stimulation and menstruation ceases. In other women the menopause occurs suddenly, menstruation remaining regular and symptomless until it ceases.

The lack of oestrogen causes atrophy of the genital tissues and a decrease in the anabolism of many others. There is sometimes thinning of the skin and loss of the protein matrix from the bones, but these changes are probably due less to oestrogen deficiency than to the ageing process itself. There is not necessarily any change in the sexual feelings. It is said that in extreme old age Ninon de l'Enclos, the famous French courtesan, asked by her grand-daughter 'Grandmama, when does a woman cease to feel the pangs of love?' replied 'My dear, I do not yet know.' Indeed many women appear to enjoy sexual intercourse more in middle-age than in youth, perhaps because there is no longer the fear of pregnancy.

Nevertheless, a number of unpleasant symptoms may occur at this time in a minority of women. The women may be the subject of 'hot flushes' and attacks of sweating, the cause of which is unknown. It used to be thought that they were due to the excessive output of gonadotrophin from the pituitary, still 'attempting' to increase the activity of ovaries no longer responsive. This cannot be the explanation, for flushes do not occur in women without ovarian tissue and with a high output of gonadotrophin; nor do they occur under treatment with gonadotrophin in either sex, and they can be controlled by doses of oestrogen too small to depress the pituitary output. In some way not understood, oestrogens must exert a stabilising influence over the peripheral circulation. The flushes are often most annoying during the night, disturbing sleep. Happily, they are readily controlled by hormonal treatment. It is important, however, not to reduce them below a tolerable level, for if they cease entirely they return when treatment is stopped. Many women never suffer in this way.

In association with hot flushes, various emotional symptoms may occur, but in a minority of women, and usually in those with an originally neurotic temperament.

It is important to realise that sixteen per cent of women simply stop menstruating, for many of them a welcome relief, and experience no menopausal symptoms whatever. Only ten per cent are incapacitated sufficiently to need treatment. The symptoms reported are flushes (62%), headache (45%), occasional vertigo (40%), increasing weight (34%), moodiness (31%), rheumatic pains (24%) and floodings (21%). These symptoms occur most often at the age of 50, but eight per cent acquire them earlier than 40 and five per cent after 55. There is no known reason why a few women should have these symptoms severely and a few not at all. Marriage or celibacy, childbirth or infertility, previous good health or bad, affect the issue not at all. One theory does, however, affect it. In Montaigne's words: 'Who feareth to suffer, suffereth already because he feareth.' The late Joan Malleson quoted one old woman who said: 'I have had a lot of trouble in my time and most of it never happened.'

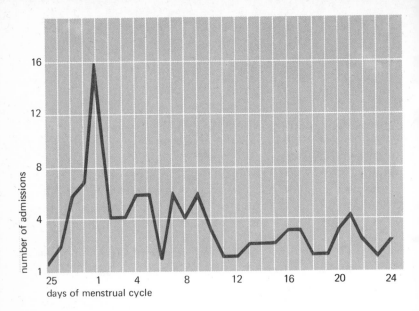

During and after the climacteric several disorders may occasionally appear or be accentuated. Obesity may occur because of decreased metabolism if the woman continues to eat as much as in her more active youth. Arthritis may result from this or from the general effects of age. Diabetes mellitus may first occur then, for a reason still unknown. Osteoporosis, manifest at this time of life, has already been mentioned. These ailments are relatively uncommon and their relationship to the climacteric is still unsure.

Perhaps the most important single fact about the 'change of life' is that in many women it is symptomless, and in the majority it causes merely trivial symptoms. In those few whose symptoms are severe, skilled hormonal treatment is invariably successful.

The premenstrual syndrome

About a third of women suffer from symptoms, at their best annoying and at their worst incapacitating, during a few days

9·6 The effect of the menstrual cycle on suicide rates. A similar graph could be drawn to illustrate the effects of the menstrual cycle on crime, accident prevalence and psychological disorders of many kinds.

107

(from one to ten) before each menstrual period. Occasionally the symptoms occur at the time of ovulation, during menstruation, or for a day or two thereafter. Sometimes they occur invariably at these times and their association with the sexual rhythm is obvious. Although, if they occur, it is always at one or other of these times, more often they do not necessarily occur at such times or may occur sometimes at one such time and sometimes at another. The association with the sexual rhythm is then not obvious even to the patient herself, and may be detected only if a careful diary is kept. A woman may experience symptoms at intervals varying from roughly a fortnight to several months, but the interval is a multiple of about a fortnight. Attacks at the time of ovulation are usually of short duration. When, as in the commonest variant of the disorder, they occur premenstrually, they continue until menstruation begins. In such cases, the attacks are prolonged if menstruation is delayed, maybe for several weeks. Almost always dramatic relief occurs at the onset of the flow and often a diuresis heralds relief.

Often too the patient is conscious of passing less urine during the time of suffering, accompanied by obvious signs of fluid retention such as swelling of the ankles or abdomen, tightness of the wedding ring, and 'puffiness' of the eyelids.

The symptoms of the premenstrual syndrome vary greatly. The commonest are psychological, though not necessarily psychogenic. The patient feels tense, depressed, lethargic, nymphomaniacal, over-anxious or irritable. Her temper may be bad enough to threaten the stability of her marriage, or cause her dismissal from her post. She may be excessively prone to accidents, to the commission of crimes of violence, or to suicide. Her soma may show the effects of the disorder more clearly than her psyche: she may suffer from a severe exaggeration of that mammary discomfort which most women notice premenstrually, or she may have rashes, asthma, obstruction of the nasal airway, dizziness, extreme hunger, increased capillary fragility, decreased sweating, nausea and vomiting, backache, epilepsy (when predisposed), or exacerbation of glaucoma.

Headache, sometimes amounting to typical migraine, is common. The pain may be bifrontal, hemicranial, bitemporal, between the eyes, over or behind one or both eyes, occipital or vertical.

Happily the premenstrual syndrome can be relieved, either by tranquilising drugs or diuretics in milder cases or by hormonal treatment in the more severe.

Infertility

The population of the world is said to be about three thousand million and at its present rate of increase it is likely to double within our lifetime. The rate of increase is likely to accelerate, not only because of a rising birth rate but because of a falling wastage of young lives and a longer expectation of life. The days of our age are no longer three score years and ten. Men are now so strong that they live to four score years (and more) and for them the problem is to prevent their strength from being a labour and sorrow that profiteth not. Humanity demands that we should continue to aid the old and thus to exaggerate the problem. At the other end of the scale the problem becomes a more individual one. A woman should have the right to decide whether she shall breed or not.

For pregnancy to occur a number of conditions must be

fulfilled. The pituitary must regulate the function of the ovary, its production both of oestradiol and progesterone and of the ova. Secondly, the ovum must be expelled from the ovary, be embraced by the fimbriae – the tasselled ends of the fallopian tubes leading to the uterus – and must thence be conducted gently to its meeting with the approaching army of eager spermatozoa. The process of ovulation occurs usually at the middle of the menstrual cycle. At other times the woman is relatively infertile, a fact which explains 'the safe period', and allows her to make use of the only method of contraception that has the blessing of the Vatican. The life of an ovum is probably not more than forty-eight hours and of a spermatozoon only two hours.

Thirdly, the fertilised ovum must become embedded in the endometrium, which can only occur when the uterus is normal and its lining properly prepared for its reception by the flood of progesterone occurring at the time of ovulation. A proper endocrine balance is necessary to maintain the right conditions in the endometrium in which the fertilised ovum may develop in the next nine months into the mature foetus. Although a proper production of progesterone, at first by the ovary and later by the placenta, is necessary to these conditions, it is probable that a common cause of failure is a defect in the germ plasma, the body tending in a way still not understood to discard a foetus doomed to be abnormal. Much has been written about the possible role of the adrenals and the thyroid in maintaining a proper environment for the developing foetus, but this has probably been exaggerated and it is doubtful whether in practice the administration of adrenal or thyroid hormone can affect the course of pregnancy.

In advising an infertile couple the doctor accepts a considerable responsibility. It may be necessary for him to advise that, because of the illness of the potential father or mother, the situation should be accepted and adoption considered. If no bar to procreation is evident, the next step is the examination of the husband, for this is simple. An ordinary clinical examination and an expert examination of his semen are all that are needed. Only if these give normal results should the far more complex investigation of the wife be begun. In a book intended for the layman it would be inappropriate to describe this in detail. From the endocrine point of view the most important part of the investigation ultimately becomes the answer to the question 'Is she ovulating?'

In this field recent advances have been dramatic chiefly owing to the expert work of Dr Gemzell in Uppsala and Dr A.C.Crooke and his colleagues in Birmingham, dramatic enough indeed to achieve headlines in the popular press. The use of human gonadotrophins has been shown to produce ovulation in many women who do not habitually ovulate and are in consequence sterile. The success rate for the production of ovulation has been put at eighty per cent and the pregnancy rate at fifty per cent. From the beginning multiple pregnancies have been the main risk. In Dr Gemzell's original series, half his successful patients had twins and one woman would have had seven children had she not aborted early. Dr Crooke's success in avoiding this hazard seemed high until the recent much advertised case of the Birmingham mother who produced six children at a birth. There seems no doubt that the problem will soon be solved.

Meanwhile another method is having some success, the use of the drug clomiphene. Whereas Dr Crooke's treatment depends on extracts from human pituitaries obtained at necropsy and is fantastically expensive, clomiphene is available on prescription, does not require expensive and expert biochemical control and appears to have no unwanted effects. In carefully selected patients, those who do not ovulate but are otherwise normal, the success rate is perhaps as high as fifty per cent.

Contraception

The prevention of pregnancy by endocrine means is a subject of enormous sociological, psychological and religious importance and controversy. It also affords an excellent example of the manner in which manipulation of the endocrine balance can effect the welfare of individuals and nations.

Whatever our views on the larger questions may be, there is no doubt that oral contraception by means of 'the pill' really works. There are probably about a million women regularly using it in Britain alone. Reports show that among these the chance of pregnancy is less than one in 100 woman years, whereas with the 'Dutch cap' and jelly the rate is three to ten and with the vaginal pessary sixteen to forty. In other words, if a woman uses 'the pill' for twenty years of her life, the chance of her becoming pregnant is less than two in a thousand and perhaps only two in 10,000, a proportion amounting to a near certainty on any well conducted race course.

The way in which 'the pill' works is still not completely certain. There are about twenty different kinds available. Most of them consist of a mixture of an oestrogen (with an action like that of oestradiol) and a progestogen (with an action like that of progesterone). The oestrogens and progestogens used are synthetic and are derived from simpler chemicals derived from the Mexican yam. The aim is to prevent ovulation. The combination appears to prevent the output from the pituitary of the luteinising hormone, allowing the continued secretion of the follicle stimulating hormone. The oestrogenic component prevents ovulation and the progestogen prevents the continued build-up of the endometrium to an inconvenient degree. The end of administration causes the shedding of the endometrium and a virtually normal 'period'. The progestogen also causes the cervix or neck of the womb to produce a sticky mucus through which the spermatozoa cannot swim.

There are several possible hazards in the continued use of 'the pill' but they are probably negligible in most women when compared with the hazards of not using it.

The hazard most widely advertised is that of increasing the clotting capacity of the blood throughout the body, with a consequent risk of thrombosis, the formation of a clot in one or other of the smaller arteries or in veins. The Committee on Safety of Drugs has concluded that the risk of thrombosis during one year's treatment is probably about the same as that of a pregnancy. The risk in a healthy woman taking the pill is about 1·3 in 100,000 in women between 20 and 34 and 3·4 in 100,000 in women between 35 and 44. The clot may occur in the arteries or veins of the lung, the heart, the brain or elsewhere. It is true that the risk of clotting is slightly greater in women using 'the pill' than in other non-pregnant women and it is therefore important that any woman known to have a greater risk anyway should avoid its use.

It seems likely that the clotting tendency is due to the oestrogenic component of the pill. The oestrogens in the blood are higher in pregnancy and it is in pregnancy that clotting is more likely to occur. It is slightly more likely to occur in women in whom lactation has been stopped by the use of stilboestrol, a synthetic oestrogen. A lesser risk is that 'the pill' has been found to produce changes in the blood similar to those found in steroid diabetes, the type of diabetes due to an overacting adrenal cortex or to excessive treatment with cortisone. It would seem wise to be cautious if a diabetic family history exists. Moreover, changes in the fatty parts of the blood suggesting a shift from a female to a male pattern have been detected and it is theoretically possible that a tendency to arteriosclerosis, always greater in men than in women, may be increased. Nevertheless as one statistician has pointed out, it is refreshing to know that it is safer to take 'the pill' than to drive a car or go to bed without it.

If, as seems likely, it is the oestrogenic component that is at fault, hope rests in experiments now going on with a purely progestogenic pill. Small doses of synthetic progestogen taken continuously may prove to be more effective. This apparently does not interfere with the output of pituitary hormones, with menstruation, or with ovulation, and its mode of action is still somewhat obscure: it may be related to its effect on the cervical mucous secretion which becomes hostile to spermatozoa, to its effect on the endometrium, which remains thin and inhospitable to the fertilised ovum, to an inhibition of the formation of the corpus luteum in the ovary, or to some other effect. Experiments are also in progress on the use of injections of a long-acting progestogen given at intervals of a month or even more.

There are other unwanted effects of 'the pill' less serious than thrombosis. Headache tends to occur and sufferers from migraine may be subject to more frequent and severe attacks. Nausea, pain in the breasts, cramp, undue fatigue, vaginal discharge, are occasionally reported but they usually disappear with continued use. Fluid retention, again probably due to the oestrogenic component, may cause increasing weight. There is no evidence of any increased risk of cancer. Conversely there is some evidence that the depression and loss of libido of which some women complain may be related to the progestogenic component.

For patients whose reaction to 'the pill' is bad, there remain the old fashioned methods or an intrauterine device usually called IUD, now used by many millions of women.

The idea is an old one, known, it is said, to Hippocrates, but the method was not commonly used until 1929 when Gräfenberg reported on 2,000 insertions into the uterus of silver rings. The method fell into disuse because of the frequency of complications and its occasional failure, though the story of a baby born dead with a Gräfenberg ring round its neck is certainly apocryphal. In the last few years the method has been revived, with plastic materials substituted for silver. Some women extrude the device and others suffer from abnormal bleeding or from pain, but for most it would so far appear to be a harmless and effective preventative of undesired pregnancy. The mode of action is unknown, but recent work on monkeys suggests that the development of the ovum within the uterus is impeded.

Perhaps the time is near when the avoidance of pregnancy will become again the duty of the man.

Knowledge of the progenitive function of the testes goes back to prehistoric times. It is probable that what we now call their endocrine function was dimly known from a date almost as remote.

One of the ancient Gods of Phrygia was Attis, perhaps the counterpart of Adonis of the Syrians and the west. Born of a virgin, he was greatly loved by Cybele, the mother of the gods and the goddess of fertility. For a reason which is somewhat obscure he died from loss of blood after castrating himself beneath a pine tree, and thereafter his priests, with a touching loyalty, felt bound to perform upon themselves a similar operation, and the custom spread in space to Rome and in time into history. In the time of the Republic the un-sexed priests of Attis were a familiar sight, marching in procession behind the image of Cybele and showered with alms and with roses by the excited populace. The Emperor Claudius, setting an example later followed in many respects by the early Christians, incorporated the Phrygian custom into the established religion of the Roman Empire. On 22 March a pine tree swathed in flowers was carried through the streets. On the next day nothing more horrifying occurred than the blowing of trumpets. On the third day, the Day of Blood, to the sound of barbaric music, the inferior clergy, whirling in a wild dance and apparently insensible to pain, gashed their bodies with knives and potsherds, splattered the sacred tree with blood and sacrificed their virility, dashing their severed organs against the image of Cybele, who, thus impregnated, hastened the resurrection of nature in the spring. Eunuch priests came to serve many goddesses in ancient times, among them Artemis of Ephesus and Astarte of Hierapolis, to whose sanctuary came pilgrims from all the eastern world, many of whom, in what we would now regard as an excess of religious fervour, castrated themselves before her shrine. It seems likely that the castration of choristers at the Vatican, continued into almost modern times and generally believed to have been performed with the natural object of preserving their soprano voices, owes its true origin to these ancient rites. The practice of castration of choristers was ended at last by Pope Leo XIII.

Even in modern times the practice of castrating boys for service in Moslem harems continued. It is often thought that the practice arose from the desire of their Moslem masters to prevent them from taking liberties with the ladies of the harem. In fact this was not so, intercourse, it is said, having been not only often possible but actually encouraged. Rather the master wished to ensure that any offspring were his own. These eunuchs have often risen to positions of trust and power, and the histories of Rome, Persia, India and China contain many examples of their influence and capacity in public affairs. Justinian's general, Narses, is a good instance of this. Voluntary castration in order to avoid sexual temptation and allow more time for the worship of the gods, the most famous example being that of Origen, has always occurred and was encouraged by St Matthew: 'there be eunuchs which have made themselves eunuchs for the kingdom of heaven's sake.' Unfortunately their ambitions must sometimes have been disappointed if their sexual instincts had already been implanted. This doubt may have been in the mind of St Augustine when he wrote: 'The Valesii castrate themselves and their guests, *thinking* thereby to serve God.'

Much of our knowledge of the effects of castration comes from the Russian religious sect of the Skoptsi, whose known history goes back only to 1771, when its leaders Ivanov and Selivanov were sent to Siberia for persuading thirteen other peasants to castrate themselves as an act of salvation. Selivanov escaped and returned to lead his people under the self-assumed title of God of Gods and King of Kings. He died in 1832 at the age of 100, but though persecuted the sect survived and flourished.

Early knowledge of the endocrine function of the testes is less than that of its function of producing spermatozoa, but it is certain that from very early times the hope of a magical sexual virility led to the practice of eating the testicles of one's enemies or of animals, like the bull, notable for their sexual prowess. The complete failure of this attempt at endocrine therapy has never, to the present day, been recognised by all, for 'fool'd with hope, men favour the deceit' and continue to waste considerable wealth on the testicular extracts of the hormone mongers.

In chimpanzees, castration in infancy does not prevent copulation in adult life, though it prevents the ejaculation of semen, which can be restored by the injection of testicular hormone. In boys, the effects are variable, and it seems likely that the lack of the hormone prevents the development of sexual interest rather than the capacity to fulfill it. In adults also the effects are variable. It is possible that the male hormone secreted by the adrenal cortex may prevent the diminution in desire and performance in some individuals, but it seems more likely that both libido and capacity, once present, come to depend more on the function of the higher centres of the brain, the hypothalamus and the autonomic nervous system than on that of the testes.

The hormone of the testes is testosterone and it is secreted by the cells of Leydig, or interstitial cells, which lie between the tubules in which the spermatozoa are formed. It is, like the hormones of the adrenal cortex, chemically a steroid.

Other steroids of testicular origin have been identified, but their functions are unknown. The members of the group are known as androgens, which means substances necessary to the maintenance of the external appearances of masculinity, the development of muscles and bones into the masculine shape, the growth of hair in a masculine distribution, the coarsening of the skin from the smooth and soft appearance typical of children and young women, the enlargement of the penis and scrotum, and the breaking of the voice. The androgens produce also more general effects. They cause an increased formation of protein from fat, particularly in muscle and bone, and in consequence an increase in their length. They cause retention of nitrogen, phosphorus and potassium. The effect of androgens on growth is of the greatest clinical importance and will be discussed more fully in chapter 21. They have also, in patients deficient in testicular function, a profound psychological effect which will be described in chapter 12. It cannot be stressed too strongly that they have no effect unless a deficiency exists. It is probably true that most of the testosterone in use is prescribed in an attempt to alleviate impotence of psychological origin, an attempt foredoomed to failure, for you cannot put more than a pint into a pint pot. On the other hand the results of treatment in the patient who has a true deficiency are brilliant. It is a sad fact that the eunuchoid boy often goes undiagnosed, accumulating often with the passage of the years a succession of psychological traumata that time can never wholly heal. His plump narrow hairless body, soft skin, weak muscles and unbroken voice single him out from amongst his schoolfellows at an age when he most desires to be one of the herd and fears to be egregious. Vaguely at first, and later poignantly, he realises that he is excluded from the erotic experiences proper to youth and that the unerring instinct of the young female places him in a different category below that of his companions. Such boys, if diagnosed before the middle teens, may be saved much misery. Their physical and emotional development may be directed into normal pathways, so that they grow to manhood subject only to one handicap, their possible inability to breed. Diagnosed later, less but still much can be done: their beard and body hair can be made to grow, although perhaps somewhat sparsely, their muscles to develop, their voices to break and their penes to enlarge and to function. But the sense of inferiority already acquired is difficult to shed and psychogenic impotence may survive the removal of its cause.

Impotence

It seems unlikely that testosterone exercises more than a slight influence over male potency. The male castrated in his youth, like one born with testicular deficiency, rarely develops sexual desire. It may be that testosterone is necessary for the development of the mind in this respect, for the man castrated in later life is not necessarily lacking in either desire or potency. Nevertheless, the middle-aged man who finds his potency diminishing is sometimes found to have a deficiency output of male hormone, and in such cases (and such cases only) treatment with testosterone may be helpful. One cannot exclude the possibility that the results are due to suggestion. The younger man whose testicles have been removed or destroyed by accident may be helped by hormonal therapy. It may be that testosterone has a 'permissive' effect, the castrates who are potent deriving sufficient for their needs from their adrenals.

The commonest cause of impotence is sexual anxiety. Erection of the penis is a parasympathetic activity easily abolished by an excess of sympathetic activity due to fear, anxiety or guilt. Such patients may occasionally be helped by advice and reassurance: psychoanalysis is useless. Nevertheless, one is left with a 'hard core' of men whose output of male hormone is normal and who appear to have no psychological cause for their impotence. Some of these are diabetic and are presumed to be suffering from diabetic neuropathy, which is unfortunately irreversible. It may be that the impotent man who is apparently psychologically and endocrinologically normal has some neurological fault so far unlocated. Hope has been aroused by the production in recent years of drugs that block the activity of the sympathetic nervous system. Some of the drugs used in the treatment of high blood pressure, those that block both the sympathetic and parasympathetic nervous systems, cause impotence, whereas those that block the sympathetic only leave potency untouched. It may be that a method will be found of stimulating the parasympathetic and suppressing the sympathetic, mimicking in this way the autonomic balance of 'paradoxical sleep', in which penicle erection often occurs.

Meanwhile, the best approach to this common problem seems to be the correction of testicular deficiency if this exists while attempting to allay anxiety, with its accompanying sympathetic overactivity, by sedatives and wise instruction.

Infertility

In order that conception may occur certain conditions must apply. Most causes of male sterility are relative rather than absolute. In the first place the testicles must produce normal spermatozoa in normal amounts. This activity is controlled initially by the anterior pituitary and its secretion of FSH. Because of pituitary deficiency the testicles may fail to develop properly or, having developed, fail to maintain their function later on.

In the second place, the testicles themselves may fail despite all that the pituitary can do about it. They may be damaged by accident, by mumps in adult years (curiously enough mumps rarely affects the testicles before puberty), by tumours, syphilis, tuberculosis or x-ray therapy. They degenerate in old age. They may be damaged by certain drugs, especially quinine and the sulphonamides.

Though they may produce normal spermatozoa, these may fail to reach their goal because of blocking of their pathway by local infection, especially gonorrhoea, by maldevelopment of the ducts, by malformations of the urethra, which may cause the sperm to be shot backwards into the bladder, or, it is claimed, by hostility of the secretion of the female genital tract. The penis itself may be malformed and fail to convey spermatozoa, or the partners may fail to reach a sufficient degree of contact because of obesity, hip disease, impotence of the male or just bad technique.

The sperms themselves may be deficient in numbers, abnormal in size or shape, or unduly lethargic. Often no cause for this is detectable. The commonest cause is probably too hot an environment. Though the secretion of FSH by the pituitary is sometimes faulty, the production of spermatozoa with a normal pituitary stimulation may be deficient because of too high a temperature. The testicles are normally maintained at a temperature about 2°C below body temperature. Men who wear underpants designed in such a way that the testicles are permanently in close contact with the body often produce few spermatozoa. Varicose veins in the scrotum, the so-called varicoceles, act as radiators of heat and are common causes of low production of sperm. Retention of the testicles within the abdomen often produces permanent degeneration of the germinal epithelium, which sets in at about the seventh year of life.

An abnormality of the spermatozoa in quantity or quality may rarely be repaired by human gonadotrophin, and the treatment has hitherto proved disappointing. Testosterone has been extensively used, but it usually causes an actual drop in the sperm count. The drop may be succeeded by a rebound when treatment ceases but not to fertile levels.

Accurate diagnosis of the cause of male infertility is therefore necessary, but it must be admitted that often this cannot be made and that even when it is treatment is rarely effective. The most hopeful cause is the presence of a varicocele, the surgical correction of which is often effective.

Maldescent of the testicle

Normally the testicles descend into the scrotum between the sixth month of intrauterine life and the first of independent existence. Their failure to do so may be due to anatomical abnormalities or to endocrine deficiency. One must differen-

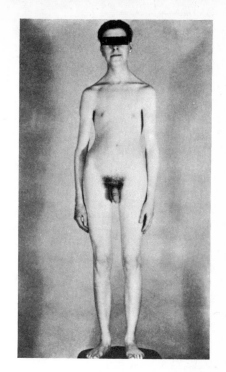

10·2 A congenital eunuch. Note the narrow shoulders, broad pelvis, feminine distribution of pubic hair, deficient muscles and hairless face. His great height (6 ft 5 ins) is due to the late union of his epiphyses, so that he continued to grow beyond the usual age.

tiate clearly between, on the one hand, what are known as retractile testicles, which sometimes occupy the scrotum, especially in warm surroundings, and sometimes retreat into the abdomen, especially during medical examination; and, on the other hand, the testicle which never descends of its own accord, the true undescended testicle. The first needs no treatment. The second needs early treatment, for the cells producing spermatozoa begin to deteriorate early in life, probably before the seventh birthday, and the degeneration is irreversible.

The testicle may lie in its normal route of descent or it may take the wrong turning. In the former case endocrine treatment is usually successful and it cannot be begun too early. In the second case, surgery is necessary and should be instituted at the age of five or six and not left, as it often is, until the age of puberty, by which time degeneration is almost certain to have occurred.

Much unnecessary controversy among doctors has gone on about the treatment of the undescended testicle. It has been claimed, perhaps with truth, that the testicle that will descend when treated with hormones will eventually descend anyway. Meanwhile not only is degeneration occurring in the testicle but a great deal of worry is experienced by the parents and ragging at school by the boys. Treatment with chorionic gonadotrophin should be begun early. If the testicle descends, all is well. What matter if it would eventually have descended of its own accord? If it does not, surgery should follow soon.

11 Hormones of the placenta, kidneys and digestive tract

The placenta

The placenta is the organ formed within the uterus when the fertilised ovum becomes attached to the lining of the uterus, the endometrium. It is responsible for the nutrition of the developing foetus and in addition secretes hormones necessary for the continuance of pregnancy. It assumes this function early in pregnancy, taking over from the anterior pituitary. It produces chorionic gonadotrophin, a protein hormone similar to pituitary gonadotrophin, which stimulates the secretion of progesterone and oestrogen by the corpus luteum of the ovary. At about three months, however, it assumes itself the secretion of these hormones This is the critical moment at which abortions often occur, should the placenta fail to assume its responsibility in time. Thereafter all the progesterone and much of the oestrogen necessary to the developing foetus is produced by the placenta. The placental hormones are necessary also for the development of the breasts during pregnancy, the oestrogen stimulating the growth of ducts and the progesterone that of the alveoli, the secreting part of the mammary glands.

These hormones alone, however, are not capable of producing full development of the breasts. A third hormone is necessary, placental lactogen. Apart from its action on the mammary glands, it has an activity similar to that of growth hormone, to which it is chemically similar. There is some hope that this hormone might be used in the treatment of dwarfism; to stimulate protein anabolism in severely ill or damaged patients; to prevent abortion; and, by stimulating the division of cancer cells, to assist in the treatment of malignant disease by radiotherapy or cytotoxic drugs, for it is in the stage of division that these cells are most easily killed.

One of the placental hormones is oestriol, a near relation of the ovarian oestradiol. The measurement of the amount of oestriol in the urine of pregnant women is a sensitive indicator of the well-being of the foetus and the placenta that nourishes it. A subnormal level is a signal that the foetus is in danger and likely to be still-born, but its premature delivery is likely to save its life.

The kidneys

The role of the kidney as an endocrine organ has been over-shadowed by its more obvious function as the main organ of excretion of the waste products of the body.

The observations that began to arouse interest in the hormones of the kidney were made mostly in the present decade. Although pathologists have been aware for a long time that in high blood pressure the adrenal glands were often enlarged, it has only recently been shown that the kidney exercises an important control over the secretion of aldo-sterone (see chapter 4) by means of what is known as the renin-angiotensin system.

The renin-angiotensin system is affected by several circum-stances. Any reduction in the volume of the blood, such as is produced by a low intake of sodium or by haemorrhage, activates the system. Even a change in posture does this. The renin output of the kidneys in a standing patient is double that of the recumbent patient. The output is increased in pregnancy, in the disease known as malignant hypertension, and by obstruction of the renal blood vessels.

Renin is produced by specialised cells in the kidneys, but it does not directly influence the production of aldosterone. After release into the blood it comes into contact with a substance, angiotensinogen, produced by the liver, catalysing the formation of angiotensin I. This, by enzyme action, is converted into angiotensin II and this, travelling in the blood to the adrenal cortex, stimulates the production of aldosterone, to a lesser extent of corticosterone, and to a slight extent of cortisol. The increased production of aldosterone corrects the low blood volume or low sodium content that has stimulated the outflow of renin, another example of the feedback mechanism so often met with in endocrinology. Angiotensin has, in addition, a direct pressor effect on the muscle of the arteries, an obviously useful one after severe haemorrhage.

Another hormone found in the kidney is erythropoietin, which regulates the production of red cells. It is released in response to anaemia. The amount entering the blood is inversely proportional to the degree of anoxia, the shortage of oxygen, in the tissues of the body. It is a glycoprotein, though its exact structure is still unknown. It is not yet certain whether it is actually produced in the kidney or just stored there. It can probably be produced in other tissues, for patients whose kidneys have been removed and who are maintained on artificial kidney machines are found to produce erythropoietin again after a few months.

Erythropoietin produces its effect by stimulating the primitive precursors of the red cells in the bone marrow. One particular kind of anaemia is associated with a deficiency of the hormone, the anaemia of chronic renal disease, but it is possible that it is involved in the anaemias of cancer, chronic infection and rheumatoid arthritis. An excess of erythropoietin is apparently involved in the excess of red cells (polycythaemia) sometimes found in malignant disease.

Yet another hormone of the kidney is called urokinase. It

11·1 The endocrine production of high blood pressure.

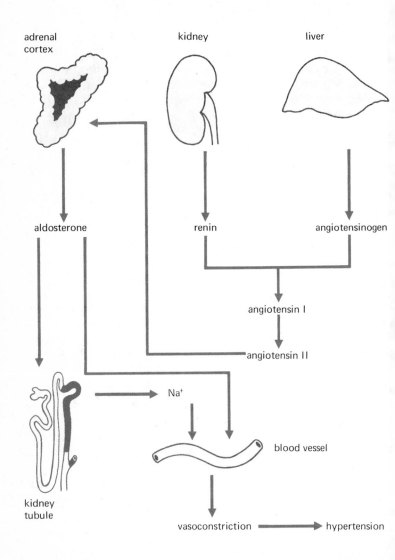

is an anti-clotting agent and may perhaps be looked at as a protection against the urinary tract becoming blocked by a blood clot. One day it may have a place in medicine as a solvent of blood clots elsewhere.

The digestive tract

The hormones of the digestive tract were the first to be recognised as such. As early as 1902 Bayliss and Starling discovered secretin and coined the word 'hormone' to describe the group of chemical messengers to which secretin belongs. Nevertheless, the digestive hormones have never elicited the same interest as other hormones, the effects of excess or deficiency of which are more dramatic. Important though they are in the regulation of digestion in health, there is only one well-recognised disease attributable to the excess of any one of them and none associated with their deficiency.

No less than eleven digestive hormones have been described; secretin, pancreozymin, enterogastrone, urogastrone, duodenin, incretin, anthelone, gastrin, villikinin, enterocrinin and cholecystokinin. The very existence of some of these and the real importance of others are in doubt. The most important in the present state of our knowledge are gastrin and secretin.

Fat is absorbed in the duodenum and the first part of the jejunum. The first stage of its digestion is the thorough mixing it undergoes in the stomach. It is then released into the duodenum, the rate of release being controlled by the hormone enterogastrone. When fat or sugar enter the duodenum, gastric acidity and motility are reduced. This effect can be produced when the hormone is administered by injection. In the duodenum the process continues, the fat being mixed here

Source	Hormone	Site of activity	Action
duodenum	secretin	pancreas	increase in alkaline juice
		liver	increase in insulin secretion
	enterogastrone	stomach	reduced mobility
			reduced acid secretion
	pancreozymin	pancreas	increase in alkaline juice
			increase in insulin secretion
	cholecystokinin	gall bladder	contraction
pylorus	gastrin	stomach	increase in acid secretion
		pancreas	increase in insulin secretion

with secretions of the liver, pancreas and the small intestine itself. These secretions are controlled by four hormones: gastrin, secretin and pancreozymin stimulate the production of pancreatic juice; secretin also increases the production of bile by the liver; and cholecystokinin causes contraction of the gall bladder and the discharge of bile into the intestine.

Gastrin is secreted by the glands of the pylorus, the passage between the stomach and duodenum. It is a very strong stimulant to the secretion of acid in the stomach, perhaps through the intermediation of histamine. Even when administered by injection it produces a profuse flow of strongly acid juice. It has recently been shown that it is present in excess in the curious syndrome of multiple endocrine tumours, the Zollinger-Ellison syndrome. In this condition vast quantities of very acid gastric juice are continuously secreted in response to an excessive production of gastrin by a tumour of the pancreas. In consequence ulcers develop in the stomach and small intestine and in addition to the well-known symptoms of ulcers the patient has profuse chronic diarrhoea. Gastrin has been studied more intensively than the other digestive hormones and has even been synthesised.

Secretin, despite its historical position as the first of all hormones, has been studied less intensively. It is secreted by the duodenum in response to a flow of hydrochloric acid from the stomach and causes a profuse flow of alkaline pancreatic juice. This neutralises the acidity of the gastric juice on entry and provides in addition the enzymes necessary for the digestion of fat and carbohydrate. Secretin has been produced in crystalline purity and produces the same effect when it is injected intravenously, thus qualifying for the title of hormone. For many years it was considered to have no other use, but as usual in endocrinology, the story proved to be too simple. It has recently been shown that secretin, gastrin and pancreozymin stimulate the production of insulin, though this action is of doubtful significance. As we have seen, pancreozymin, also secreted in the duodenum, stimulates the production of pancreatic juice, and cholecystokinin, by causing the gall bladder to pour out bile, aids the digestion of fat. The other digestive hormones may be left in obscurity.

Part 2

Hormone effects on body functions

12 The nervous system and behaviour

The relationship between hormones and the nervous system is so close that the famous physiologist John Fulton once remarked that endocrinology was a branch of neurology. We have seen in earlier chapters that the hypothalamus, an integral part of the nervous system, produces hormones that control the production of pituitary hormones – the so-called releasing factors. It also produces the hormones believed in the past to be produced by the posterior pituitary, where in fact they are merely stored. The hypothalamus has ousted the anterior pituitary from its old pride of place. Another link is provided by the catecholamines, for as we have seen these are produced not only by the adrenal medulla but at the nerve endings of the autonomic nervous system. Moreover, the target endocrine glands, though mainly under the control of the trophic hormones of the anterior pituitary are themselves subject to some degree of autonomic control.

In various human disorders the link between the systems is so close that to ask whether a disease is neurological or endocrinological is a question without point. One of these is diabetic neuropathy in which the link up is still mysterious. The symptoms and signs vary widely. Some patients have muscle atrophy and paralysis, others merely numbness and pins and needles in their feet. There seems to be no relationship between the symptoms and the severity of the diabetes or whether or not it is being properly treated.

One of the commonest symptoms for which the neurologist is consulted is headache. It was fashionable a few decades ago to speak of a 'pituitary headache'. This diagnosis was often based on the occurrence of headache in some women during the third trimester of pregnancy, when an increase in the size of the pituitary occurs. The gland was supposed to press on the optic nerves and pain-sensitive parts.

But the increase is in fact very slight and far greater increases occur without headache. Nevertheless rapidly growing tumours of the pituitary sometimes cause severe headache and apparently this does not depend on an increase in pressure within the cranium. When headache occurs it is due to traction on veins or arteries, inflammation or stretching of pain-sensitive structures such as the dura, or direct pressure on nerves.

Disorder of the thyroid is not a common cause of headache, and when it occurs it is probably due to the muscular tension so common in thyroid overactivity. People with large goitres tend to push their heads forward and upset the mechanics of the cervical spine. In adrenal disease it is common. In Cushing's disease it is probably due to the thinning of the bones in the cervical spine which often occurs. It is an almost constant feature in cases of tumour of the medulla but the reason for this is unknown.

The most interesting, because the most common, headache due to endocrine imbalance is that from which many women suffer before their periods, sometimes amounting to attacks of classical migraine. The premenstrual syndrome has been discussed in chapter 9.

'The future may teach us to exercise a direct influence by means of chemical substances upon the amounts of energy and their distribution in the apparatus of the mind. It may be that there are undreamed of possibilities of therapy, but for the moment we have nothing better at our disposal than the technique of psychoanalysis.' Thus, in 1938, wrote the master, Sigmund Freud, with a discernment rarely shown by his disciples today. The chemical substances postulated by Freud, many of them hormones, have been the subject of intense investigation in the last thirty years or so.

Although much of the relationship between the endocrines and the mind is of recent discovery, the effects of castration on human aggressiveness were well recognised in ancient times. The first experimental verification was by Berthold of Göttingen, who changed the cock into a submissive bird by castration and restored its aggressiveness by re-implanting its testicles. That masculine aggressiveness may supplant feminine submissiveness in the presence of an adrenal tumour was first recognised by Gordon Holmes in 1925. This change is commonly seen when the proportion of oestrogens to androgens is naturally diminished in women at the menopause, and its converse is observed often in the 'mellowing' of the ageing man. These changes in character are possibly related to the effects of the sexual hormones on the hypothalamus. In the small knob of tissue called the amygdala there exists an 'aggression centre', electrical stimulation of which can turn aggressive behaviour on and off at the touch of a switch. The amygdala can be affected by sights, sounds and smells and by hormones. A raging bull can be converted into a gentle steer by castration. Aggressive behaviour in lactating female rats can be blocked by oestrogens and reactivated by androgens or cortisol. It is possible to suppress the aggression centre by the stimulation of cerebral circuits and it has even been suggested that a built-in stimulator might be used by the violent paranoid himself to control his instincts.

When two male mice meet they usually begin to fight, invariably if they have been isolated. Females and castrated males are less aggressive. If castrated males are treated with testosterone they become hostile but females so treated do not, unless they are so treated from birth. Clearly the infantile is more susceptible than the adult mind to hormonal influence, and, the Jesuits would add, to other influences as well.

Much of recent work stems from that of Selye, whose concept envisages a wide variety of stresses, each producing an effect upon the body as a whole by way of the hormones, especially those of the adrenal cortex. Amongst these stresses are shocks and more sustained strains emanating from the mind. It has been shown that the strain of public speaking, of awaiting surgical operation, of military combat, of the 'Varsity boat race, increase the concentration of cortico-steroid hormones in the blood and urine, especially, in the last example, of the coach and the cox. Emotional stress may precipitate thyrotoxicosis, exacerbate diabetes mellitus, stop or accentuate menstruation, or cause water retention by stimulation of the secretion of antidiuretic hormone. These somatic results of mental strain appear one and all to be the end results of a chain of reactions that begins in the cortex of the brain and wends its way through the hypothalamus, the pituitary gland and the target glands to the periphery. One of the most interesting questions is why some individuals are more subject to this chain of reactions than others. If this question can be answered we shall be well on the way to an understanding of the psychosomatic disorders. There is no single mental illness that is constantly associated with a single endocrine disorder. Perhaps some people spend their lives walking along a psychopathological tightrope from which they may be pushed either way by excess or deficiency of glandular function, to hit the ground with equal force which-ever way they fall. Perhaps some people are more ready than others to bring into operation their counter-stress mechan-isms. Some highly strung people may bring their mechanisms into action with undue and damaging enthusiasm, while others are so calmly made that they need not bring their mechanisms into force at all except in extreme circumstances.

The mental effects of low blood sugar provide a good example of the variety of results of a single stimulus. Some sort of mental or nervous effect is invariably seen when the blood sugar is lowered by an insulin-secreting tumour of the pancreas, in Addison's disease or in the still rather mysterious entity of 'idiopathic hypoglycaemia'. At one end of the scale are fatigue, anxiety, restlessness, irritability and a feeling of tension. In the middle lie automatic activity, confusion, loss of memory, drunken behaviour and negativism. At the other end may be seen mania, violence, hallucinations, delirium, delusions and coma. It would seem that the mental effects of low blood sugar depend not only on the actual level but on the way the brain reacts to it. Brain function depends on the availability of glucose. In one famous case a young man of unstable character whose blood sugar was low because of a prolonged fast stabbed his mother to death. One woman received prolonged psychiatric treatment for a tendency to become noisy and abusive with no provocation, until a discerning psychiatrist became suspicious and referred her to an endocrine clinic, where she was cured by the removal of a pancreatic tumour.

The pancreas is by no means the only organ the disordered functions of which can induce dementia. A low blood sugar and a low level of calcium in the blood stream may on occasions have a strangely similar effect. The fact that dementia is uncommon suggests that this abnormality of the blood chemistry, due to an 'idiopathic' reduction in the activity of the parathyroid glands or to their surgical removal, purposeful or accidental, discloses a previous mental abnormality but does not create a new one. The originally sound mind retains its balance, the unsteady one falls off its tightrope. Depression, loss of interest in surrounding things and people, lack of personal care, vertigo, anxiety and epilepsy may occur. One woman who suffered from a tumour of a parathyroid gland had the brittle bones usual in this disease. The tumour was removed and the serum calcium fell from an unduly high to an unduly low level. Although this was quickly rectified she became confused and began to suffer from strange delusions. She thought she was in Hell and that the other patients in the ward were devils sent to plague her. Her screams and curses were so disturbing to her neighbours that a psychiatrist was called in with a view to her transfer to a mental hospital. She formed the highly erroneous opinion that he was Christ, come to rescue her and escort her to Heaven. He reported that she was hopelessly and permanently insane and left the ward to make the necessary arrangements for her transfer. As he left the ward she rushed to follow him, slipped, fell heavily, and broke her still brittle femur. Within a minute she was perfectly sane, providing an interesting example of shock therapy applied by the patient herself.

Perhaps the most common mental symptom in parathyroid deficiency, even in those of good mental balance, is a profound depression that can rapidly be relieved by means of calcium. Depression also occurs when the level of potassium in the blood falls too low. This is seen in Cushing's disease due to overactivity of the adrenal cortex, but also when too little potassium is present in the diet, when vomiting is profuse, and when diuretic and purgative drugs are abused. All these conditions are commonly present in patients with abnormal personalities. Wolff and his colleagues have shown that one or more courses of events occur, as shown in figure 12·1.

Perhaps in this wildly speculative field of study the relation-

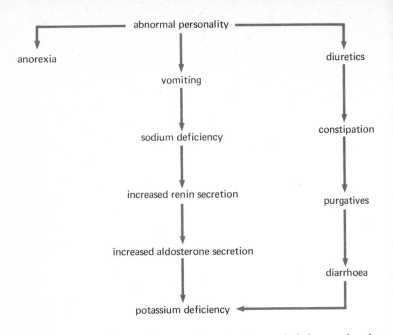

ship between depression and potassium deficiency is the nearest we can get to relating definitely a chemical (often endocrine) abnormality with a mental state. The effect of contraceptive pills in producing depression was mentioned in chapter 9.

Noradrenaline and 5-hydroxytriptamine (5 HT) are two amines normally present in the nervous system. Monoamine oxidase (MAO) is the enzyme that inactivates them. Drugs such as reserpine that inhibit these amines cause depression in animal experiments and often in man. Conversely those which inhibit MAO cause excitement in animals and have sometimes proved useful in relieving depression in patients. The use of these drugs was based on similar reasoning rather than direct proof until recently. It has now been shown that the amines are present in a subnormal concentration in the brains of depressed people and that the level is restored to normal by monoamine oxidase inhibitors.

Recently hope has been aroused that the chemistry of

12·1 Reduction of potassium in psychological disease. This may occur for many reasons. The commonest today is probably the unwise, over-prolonged and excessive use of cortisone and similar drugs in patients with no psychological disease.

141

anxiety may similarly be clarified. Pitts and McClure in America have shown that after exercise (which always raises the level of lactate in the blood) anxious patients experience an undue rise and concomitantly feelings of dread and causeless fear of, for instance, a heart attack or death. If lactate is infused into normal people until it rises to ten times the normal blood level, they experience typical attacks of anxiety that can be prevented by the simultaneous infusion of calcium. The authors advanced the hypothesis that anxiety states occur in normal people due to the blood lactate rising too high in response to an increased release of adrenaline. It is certain that many of the symptoms of anxiety can be produced by the injection of adrenaline, which may evoke a profound emotional disturbance even in normal people but especially in anxiety neurotics. Conversely, some well-balanced people may experience a pleasant thrill when slight fear in controllable circumstances raises their output of adrenaline. Perhaps this explains rock-climbers, and racing enthusiasts on horses or in motor cars.

Schizophrenia may well be of endocrine origin. Thudichum wrote in 1884: 'Many forms of insanity are unquestionably the external manifestations of the effects upon the brain substances of poisons fermented within the body. . . . These poisons we shall, I have no doubt, be able to isolate after we know the normal chemistry to its utmost detail. And then will come in their turn the crowning discoveries to which our efforts must ultimately be directed, namely, the discoveries of the antidotes to the poisons and to the fermenting causes and processes which produce them.' Mescaline is a drug which produces effects that mimic the natural disorder. Chemically it is very like adrenaline, and it has been suspected that schizophrenics may have an abnormality of adrenaline metabolism that results in the production of an abnormal metabolite with an action similar to that of mescaline. One interesting metabolite of mescaline itself is one with the terrifying name of 3,4-dimethoxyphenyl-ethylamine, usually known as DMPE. It is a dimethylated derivative of dopamine, which as we have already seen, is found in the adrenal medulla. Chromatography of the urine of schizophrenics has excitingly detected in many a pink spot which is absent from the urine of normal people. It was formerly suspected of being DMPE, but this is not so. Another curious thing about schizophrenics is that only twenty per cent of them have normal thyroid function, most of the males having a deficiency and most of the females an excess. Correction of the thyroid function causes an improvement in the mental state. How this fact is related to the rest of what we know about schizophrenia is still a mystery. In the manic-depressive psychosis it may be that the adrenal cortex is involved, for the blood of patients in a manic state has been found to prolong the life of animals whose adrenals have been removed.

The changes in weight that occur in periodic mental disease suggest endocrine involvement, for they are undoubtedly due to fluid retention. Nine pounds or so may be gained or lost in a day, deterioration in the mental state seemingly coinciding often with the days on which the weight is lowest.

The gland most closely associated in popular imagination with mental changes is the thyroid. Indeed long ago one read of the hyperthyroid and hypothyroid personalities. These do not exist. A person is either hyperthyroid or hypothyroid or has a normal thyroid level. Nevertheless there is a grain of truth in the old concept. Hyperthyroidism tends to make a patient more irritable, anxious and excitable than he previously was because of the effects already discussed of thyroxine on the autonomic nervous system. Conversely hypothyroidism slows down the autonomic nervous system and tends to make the patient slower in his emotional reactions than in the past. However the effects of too much or too little circulating thyroxine must be looked upon merely as effects upon the previous personality. The previously highly excitable person may be raised to an almost manic state should he develop thyrotoxicosis, whereas the previously phlegmatic person may be raised only to a normal level. Conversely the person previously excitable may be reduced to a normal level by deficient thyroid activity, the previously phlegmatic person becoming still more calm. The common factor is the effect of thyroxine in stimulating cerebral and autonomic activity.

Myxoedema, due to a profound drop in thyroid activity, has other effects. Far from producing a calmer outlook it may give rise to extreme irritability, perhaps due to the frustration of an active mind that realises its new incompetence. Worse things may occur. Though fully developed myxoedema is easy to diagnose even from the appearance of the patient, the diagnosis is not always so easy. There is little doubt that many cases of psychosis severe enough for incarceration in mental hospitals are due to thyroid deficiency. Such patients may remain undiagnosed and rot for years in such institutions before a perspicacious psychiatrist suddenly sees the light. The madness may take many forms. As long ago as 1888 a committee of the Clinical Society of London recorded that 'delusions and hallucinations occur in nearly half the cases, mainly where the disease is advanced. Insanity as a complication is noted in about the same proportion as

144

12·2 Myxoedematous madness.
On the right is a picture of the patient
before treatment began, on the far
right after treatment with thyroxine. After
thirteen years undiagnosed in a mental
hospital, she made a complete recovery.

delusions and hallucinations. It takes the form of acute or chronic manias, dementia, or melancholia, with a marked predominance of suspicion and self-accusation.' Paranoia and severe confusion may also occur and result in extremely violent behaviour. Should the condition go undiagnosed the damage may be permanent but even after many years as a certified lunatic a patient may be cured by thyroxine and return to a happy and useful life. In lesser degrees of psychological abnormality the presence of thyroid deficiency may be overlooked all too easily. Students are too often trained to think only of the most severe symptoms and to expect to see them altogether in every patient. In fact there is no symptom or sign of deficiency that may not be absent and in many instances only one of these may be present. That one may be a disorder of behaviour or of thought.

The cretin is an example of the effect on the brain of prolonged thyroid deficiency. Thyroxine is necessary for the development of the brain. If treatment is begun within a few weeks of birth, the cretin may progress sufficiently to grow into an adult not obviously different from his fellows, but the effects of thyroid deficiency before birth are rarely completely reversed, and he never becomes outstandingly intelligent. If the diagnosis is not made for months or years, the hope of completely normal mental development progressively recedes. The mental deficiency of the adult cretin is often strangely patchy. He may surprise one with sudden flashes of intelligence momentarily illuminating the general darkness of his mind. In general his mind is childlike, his emotions labile and uninhibited. He is often, like so many normal children, thoughtlessly cruel and spiteful, often pathetically dependent.

This book is about human hormones. Although recent history has thrown some doubt on the idea that essential

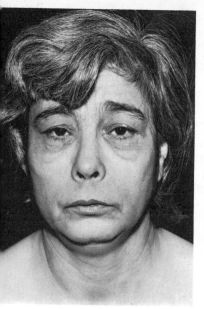

differences exist between the behavioural reactions of man and the so-called lower animals, it remains true that it is unwise to transfer from one animal to another the lessons learned. Anthropomorphism has bedevilled our observations about the behaviour of other species than our own, and the reverse statement applies. The dear old lady who attributes human instincts and thought-processes to her pekinese dog is committing in reverse the mistake of the experimental worker who extrapolates from the 'lower' primate, or even from the insect, the bird or the other mammals, to human beings. Nevertheless Cannon in the last century underlined the fact that many common features in the behaviour of other vertebrates are mediated by hormonal action and that these may occasionally be applicable to the human being.

Thus experiments have shown that dogs and cats deprived of their cerebral hemispheres are still capable of copulation and fertility. The study of the human race suggests that this is true of men and women. It may even be said that these functions are often increased in those whose cerebral capacity is low. The lordosis of the women, the palpation and pelvic thrust, the hopping and wiggling of the ears, all so typical of the female rat in a state of sexual receptivity, may be observed on any evening on any dance floor. The back-kicking of the unreceptive female rat is in such circumstances rarely observed. In male rats cerebral damage of such a degree that sexual interest dies may be repaired by the injection of testosterone. It is perhaps fortunate that this hormone fails to produce a similar effect in man. In female rats and cats on the other hand, the removal of the whole cerebral cortex fails to reduce the copulatory response and in the human species the temporary ablation of the cortex by alcohol, though it may fail to reduce the female response, may seriously impair that of the male, as the porter in *Macbeth* so correctly observed four centuries ago. It would appear that in the male the higher centres play a larger part than the endocrine in sexual behaviour, a point to which we shall return. Male apes castrated in infancy display a speed and frequency of copulation that compares favourably with the performance of the intact animal, and in the human species the eunuch is not necessarily impotent. On the other hand the removal of the ovaries from the female rat eliminates completely her sexual responses, whereas the virtual death of the ovaries in the human female in middle age does not necessarily do so.

The problems of puberty and adolescence now occupy much space in the daily press, brought to the fore by the violent and apparently insensate behaviour of students in recent demonstrations. It seems likely that the apparent causes of their misdemeanour are unimportant. The war in Vietnam, the demand for 'student power' in the government of universities, opposition to nuclear warfare, the pros and cons of racial segregation, are probably only pegs upon which the adolescent hangs his desire to be of the crowd, and to avoid the growing necessity to be an individual, lonely and responsible. Moreover the increased feeling of aggression caused by a flood of testosterone to which his brain has not yet learned to adapt itself must find an outlet. Intellectual development tends to lag behind sexual development and social development behind intellectual development. That these stages in maturation are partly of endocrine origin is suggested by animal experiments in which it has been found that castration reduces the capacity to learn of male rats, a reduction that can be corrected by testosterone. In spayed female rats oestradiol produces the opposite result and reduces their capacity to learn, an effect that can be neutralised by testosterone. To what extent these observations are relevant to man is in doubt, and the feminist would certainly deny their applicability, but one observation suggests that they have some human validity. The clinical endocrinologist sees frequently the boy who is sexually, somatically and scholastically backward. His genitalia are unduly small, his height is below the normal for his age and his form mates are younger than he. Treatment aimed at increasing his sexual development has as a by-product an acceleration of growth due to the fact that androgens have an anabolic activity. It is an almost invariable rule that the boy's scholastic achievement increases as well, often to the pleased surprise of his masters. It sometimes seems that before puberty a boy only works if forced to do so. Later the mind matures and he begins to see that work is not only necessary but even interesting.

Some of the improvement may be due to other causes. The

increased aggressiveness produced by testosterone may help. The unhappiness felt by the boy who is too small to stand up to his fellows may have been a handicap in the past. The psychological effects of being different are often underrated by doctors who assure the parents that eventually all will be well. 'Leave it to nature' is the advice most commonly given. The misery suffered is neglected: its effects may last for life.

Masturbation has almost lost its old position as a problem of puberty. It never was, initially, a problem for the boy or girl: it was made one by the parents, who adopted a puritan and hypocritical view often bolstered by the invention of strange diseases supposed to result from this normal practice. According to Kinsey, ninety per cent of American males have masturbated before they are seventeen. This is probably an underestimate. The great French neurologist Charcot remarked that if a man claimed never to have masturbated he did it still. The figures for girls are less easily found, but the practice is undoubtedly common amongst them.

Another 'problem' we tend to take too seriously is the transient homosexuality of adolescence in both sexes. Sexual feelings arise and must be satisfied. The segregation of the sexes in boarding schools is bound to lead to 'crushes' on an object of the same sex. This temporary homosexuality seems in the majority to be readily curable by the proximity of an individual of the opposite sex. In those in whom it is permanent a deeper explanation must be sought. Probably it is never glandular. Samuel Johnson defined puberty as 'the time of life when the two sexes begin to be acquainted'. The time should not be too long delayed or the acquaintance too distant.

At the other end of the span of reproductive life, the change of life or climacteric may have profound emotional effects.

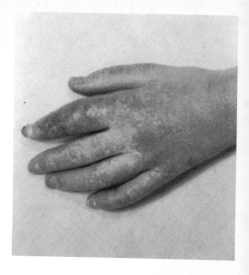

12·3 The hand in a severe case of anorexia nervosa. Malnutrition has led successively to thyroid deficiency, a very low body temperature, spasm of the peripheral arteries in an attempt to reduce heat loss, and finally gangrene. The circulation was temporarily restored by blocking of the automatic supply to the arteries by the injection of local anaesthetic, and finally restored by the cure of anorexia nervosa.

Whether there exists in the male a phase of rapidly diminishing testicular function is doubtful. Excretory studies suggest that there is a very gradual diminution in the secretion of testosterone in middle age and old age, and it is doubtful whether this is related to the psychological changes that undoubtedly occur in some elderly men. Occasionally they experience a wide variety of symptoms, such as emotional instability, irritability, sudden changes in mood, failing memory and concentration, decreased interest in their usual activities and severe depression. Yet it must be remembered that there are often sound psychological causes for these symptoms. The man in whose past life sex has been a major interest finds his attraction for women beginning to wane and his capacity for responding to it growing smaller. He may have concentrated unduly upon his work and may find it difficult to fill his days. If games once occupied his mind unduly he may be depressed by his lessening skill. As he approaches his three score years and ten he finds his friends growing fewer as death claims them. He himself may begin to fear death for his own sake or for others.

In women it is otherwise. The fall in ovarian activity is relatively sudden. The same causes of psychological symptoms may operate as in the male, but to these are added physical symptoms that may be very disturbing, such as hot flushes, attacks of excessive sweating, excessive and irregular menstrual bleeding and painful changes in the skin of the genital area. The combination of the two factors, psychological and physical, may make life unbearable for the patient and her family. Happily the symptoms in a severe form are comparatively rare. The majority of women pass through the climacteric unscathed. Happily also the symptoms in women are easily and effectively controlled by the administration of hormones (see chapter 9).

Homosexuality has been suspected of having an endocrine origin, but evidence for this view does not exist. No abnormality has ever been demonstrated in the proportion of male to female hormones in blood or urine. The male homosexual does not become heterosexual when treated with testicular hormones. Under treatment with testosterone the sex drive may be increased in either sex, but its direction is not reversed. Homosexuals reach puberty at the usual age, and physical examination of the adult shows no sign of endocrine abnormality. Moreover in people who are known to have an abnormal ratio of sex hormones, homosexuality is not unduly common.

It is often difficult to tell, in a particular set of circumstances, what is the cause and what is the effect. It has indeed been said that cause and effect are always simultaneous and that when there is a gap in time between the two it is filled with intercurrent effects. Unless A, the cause, and Z the effect, are simultaneous, there is a chain of causes and effects between the two, A causing B and B causing C until at last

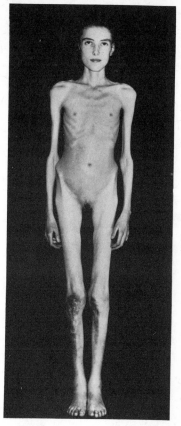

12·4 Another example of anorexia nervosa, showing the extreme degree of emaciation, reduction in pubic hair, and atrophy of the breasts.

we arrive at Z. Yet Z may be only a waiting room, the obvious effect of A, and itself the initiator of more ripples in the physiological pond.

An example of this dilemma is anorexia nervosa, the condition in which the patient, usually a young girl, decides for reasons known usually only to herself, if at all, to starve. Often the obvious (but not necessarily true) beginning is an obsessional desire to be slimmer, occasionally because mother is fat and the common mother-daughter antagonism of 'the teens' dictates a desire to be as unlike mother as it is possible to be. Usually such obvious 'causes' are undetectable.

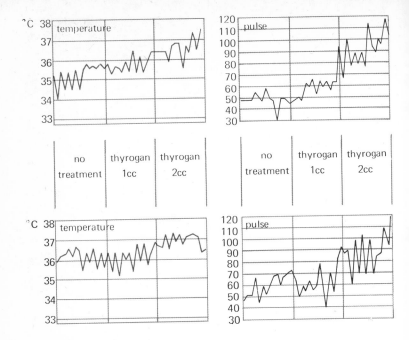

A simple explanation of the results of starvation, to which at one time I adhered, was that the desire to slim produced a protective chain reaction by way of the hypothalamus. In consequence the pituitary reduced its output of trophic hormones. First went the gonadotrophic hormones and in consequence the ovaries ceased to function, menstruation ceased, the breasts atrophied and the sexual hair diminished. The survival of the race was subjugated to the survival of the individual. Secondly went the thyroid function. This, though never totally depressed, protected the individual against the effects of starvation. The metabolic rate fell (often to levels never seen in myxoedema), so that the patient could remain alive despite the virtual absence of food. The temperature and pulse-rate fell and the skin became cold and dry. There was none of the expected rise in weight, because too little food was taken to allow this. The expected dulling of the faculties was counterbalanced by the neurotic tendencies that

12·5 The effects of thyrotrophic hormone on the temperatures and pulse rates of two patients with anorexia nervosa. These figures demonstrate the fact that in anorexia nervosa there is a functional hypopituitarism.

153

lay at the basis of the disorder. Thirdly, the adrenal function fell and it was noticeable that the production of the adrenal function concerned with the secretion of the corticotrophic hormones, dependent on pituitary control, would fall though the mineralotrophic hormones, less dependent on pituitary stimulation, remained unaffected. The glucose tolerance curve became low and flat but the salt metabolism remained normal. Ultimately however death occurred because of adrenal failure.

This hypothesis has never been disproven, but it aroused intense opposition from those who desired, for very good reasons, to distinguish between Simmonds' disease and Sheehan's disease (in which pituitary inefficiency was established) and anorexia nervosa. The two were too often confused. Yet there seems to be little doubt that in anorexia nervosa we are faced with what in effect is a functional hypopituitarism of hypothalamic origin, the hypothalamic disorder being itself of cerebral origin.

There are good reasons for the objections. The amenorrhoea of anorexia nervosa may actually precede the initiation of starvation, suggesting that hypothalamic disorder may be primary. After all, the appetite centres lie in the hypothalamus. Perhaps therefore starvation may not be the finger which fires the gun. The anorexia may be an effect of hypothalamic disorder rather than its cause. This idea does not, of course, exclude the idea that the disease is psychogenic. Examples of the effects of the psyche on menstruation were given in chapter 9. The psychogenic effects on ovarian function may go further. An excessive desire for pregnancy may, it seems, actually inhibit it. Many married women, sterile for years, become pregnant after a simple gynaecological examination, a fact that has led to some leg-pulling within the medical profession, but is clearly due simply to the relief of tension due to the burden having been cast on broader shoulders. It is possible that excessive anxiety during coitus causes contraction of the Fallopian tubes and prevents the meeting of ovum and spermatozoon.

Cushing's syndrome is often accompanied by psychological changes, even by complete insanity. I have seen a very able woman become completely insane before the diagnosis was made. By the time she came into my hands she was very fat with a red face like the full moon, excess of hair on the chin, bruises over her body, sugar in her urine, a high blood pressure and a mind completely divorced from reality. Her adrenal glands were removed and by the time she recovered from the anaesthetic she was mentally normal. Conversely the psychological effects of Addison's disease may be profound – apathy, negativism, seclusiveness, depression and irritability occur in about half the cases. Undue suspiciousness and agitation are fairly common and delusions occasionally occur.

Psychological causes are generally regarded as the commonest causes of male impotence. They have probably been exaggerated. A diminution in the output of male hormone is only occasionally found in such cases. Moreover, such a diminution does not necessarily produce impotence. Old men, in whom the excretion of male hormone is usually low, are not necessarily impotent. The famous Old Parr is said to have 'gotten a virgin with child' on his hundredth birthday. The eunuchs in eastern courts were, it is said, encouraged to have coitus with the ladies of the harem not at the time in especial favour with the master. The object of the operation to which they had been subjected was to ensure that all children born in the harem were legitimate and not to restrict the pleasure of the inmates. In a large proportion of men complaining of impotence a good psychological 'cause' may be found, usually a feeling of anxiety about their prowess, often induced by excessive demand by their wives, by an unjustifiable accusation of infidelity, or by a deflection of their libido on to another woman. In many, however, no such psychological cause is ascertainable and the most likely explanation appears to be not endocrine at all but due to autonomic imbalance. Erection of the penis is due to para-sympathetic impulses, often evident on awakening from the type of sleep associated with rapid eye movements. Many men impotent at night are potent in the early morning, but many women are unreceptive at this time. The slightest element of sexual anxiety stimulates the sympathetic side of the autonomic nervous system and creates the situation well summed up in a ribald story in which the lover was forced to the statement: 'My hair and my cock won't stand on end at the same time.' The situation is sometimes seen in the case of the young man who has for other reasons had to undergo castration. If at the time of the operation he is given an implant of testosterone and told forcibly that because of this his sexual powers will be unimpaired, all is well. If no implant is given he usually (but not always) becomes im-potent. When, months later, impotence has set in and an implant is carried out it may be ineffective. Sexual anxiety has become implanted first and is only with great difficulty overcome.

13 The cardiovascular system

The control of the heart and blood vessels is the immediate concern of the autonomic nervous system and the balance of its two parts, the sympathetic and parasympathetic. To a very large extent the effects of the various hormones are mediated by their effects on this system.

The pituitary

The hormones of the anterior pituitary appear to have no direct effects but indirectly their effects, exerted by the hormones of the target glands, the thyroid and adrenals especially, are profound. It is otherwise with those of the posterior pituitary. The role of oxytocin is still obscure. Certainly large doses cause vasodilatation in the limbs and a fall in blood pressure but whether this is of physiological importance is unknown. The importance of the other posterior pituitary hormone, vasopressin or the antidiuretic hormone (ADH) is clearer. ADH makes the distal part of the nephron (the functional unit of the kidney) more permeable to water, which is reabsorbed into the blood instead of being voided as urine. The tissues of the body would become in this way oversaturated with water and an additional strain would be imposed on the heart but for the fine balance imposed on the output of ADH from the posterior pituitary. The dilution of the blood causes an immediate diuresis, or increased output of urine, and the *status quo* is regained. This activity of ADH is obvious to the least observant. The man who has lost an excessive amount of water by sweating or has gone many hours without drinking, passes a small quantity of dark and concentrated urine. The man who has been drinking heavily in a pub passes large quantities of dilute and colourless urine. The mechanism generally works with such accuracy that health is not disturbed. When disorder of the hypothalamus causes a pathological reduction in the release of ADH the disease of diabetes insipidus, first recognised by Willis in the seventeenth century, occurs, causing a continuously excessive output of urine, extreme thirst and disturbance of sleep, the unfortunate patient spending a great part of his days and nights either passing urine or replacing water lost by drinking. The opposite condition is less well authenticated, but patients have been described in whom an unexplained oedema is associated with a high blood pressure and the presence in the urine of an antidiuretic substance which might well be vasopressin. In large doses vasopressin contracts all smooth muscle, including that of the small arteries or arterioles, and a high blood pressure would therefore be expected were the output from the posterior pituitary unduly high.

The thyroid

We have seen that the thyroid hormone thyroxine has two main functions, the regulation of the rate of oxidation in all the tissues of the body, and the 'setting' of the level of activity of the autonomic nervous system. An increase in the secretion of thyroxine causes an increase in general metabolism. This implies an increased demand for oxygen, which can only be supplied by an increase in the blood supply to every organ and therefore in the work of the heart. The increased demand for oxygen and the resultant call for rapid removal of metabolic waste products is met by increased heart rate, by dilatation of the arterial tree (which therefore not only carries more traffic but has a decreased peripheral resistance to blood flow), by an increased output of blood

from the heart, by increased velocity of blood flow, and b
an increased difference between the systolic and diastoli
blood pressures. The stimulation of the sympathetic ma
increase the heart rate to a point at which the muscle of th
heart is no longer capable of bearing the burden. Conversely
if thyroxine is secreted to a deficient extent, all tissue meta
bolism is slowed, the body is cold and the heart beats mor
slowly.

When, as in thyrotoxicosis, the output of thyroxine i
excessive, heart consciousness is often the first and mos
prominent symptom. The heart usually beats at an excessiv
pace even when the patient is asleep. In severe cases th
arhythmia known as atrial fibrillation is common: the hear
beats with a double irregularity of both rate and force. Whe
first it occurs it may do so 'on and off' in paroxysms of whicl
the patient is unpleasantly aware: later it persists. It is a
warning of impending heart failure. Until, not so long ago, i
became generally recognised that thyrotoxicosis is one of th
common causes of atrial fibrillation, the disease often wen
unrecognised. The patient was regarded as suffering from a
diseased heart and treated for this only, with fatal results
Now, treated by radioactive iodine, antithyroid drugs and
adrenergic blocking agents that stop the excessive action o
the sympathetic, the patient is almost always restored t
perfect health.

The opposite condition of myxoedema may also affect th
heart. Here the pulse rate is slow, for total metabolism is lov
and the tissues are not, as in thyrotoxicosis, avid for oxygen
In severe deficiency of thyroxine there is, as we have seen, a
tendency to retain fluid and this may occur within th
pericardium and embarrass the heart muscle. This in its turi
may share with many other tissues the tendency to becom

clogged with a mucus-like substance (hence the word myxoedema) with consequent loss of efficiency.

In myxoedema there is usually an excessive level of cholesterol in the blood stream, we know not why. It is not yet proven that a high blood cholesterol is the cause of coronary heart disease and many experts believe that it is not. Figures seem to show that lowering the level by special diets, a variety of drugs or thyroid hormone does nothing to prevent heart attacks. Nevertheless it is true that in thyroid deficiency, disease of the coronary arteries is more common than when the thyroid secretion is normal, and at the post-mortem examination of people who have died of a coronary attack many are found to have hypothyroidism, often un-recognised in life. However it has also been found that though there is a rise in the blood cholesterol of young patients whose thyroids have been totally removed, there is found at post-mortem examination no more arterial disease in general than would be expected in people of similar age. It must be admitted that the relationship between the thyroid and coronary disease and arterial degeneration is still obscure. A snag that may make diagnosis impossible is provided by the dilemma of angina pectoris, known to be caused occasionally by an excessive dose of thyroxine. It is less generally known that anginal pain may occur in the flabby and embarrassed heart of the myxoedematous patient and may be cured by the cautious use of thryoxine combined with an adrenergic-blocking drug.

The treatment of thyroid deficiency with thyroxine is usually easy, but occasionally a patient is seen whose heart is unduly sensitive to it. Doses too small to put right the metabolism, and lower the weight or the blood cholesterol or improve the sluggish mind may so speed the heart that, burdened as it is with fluid and mucus-like deposits, it becomes seriously embarrassed. Here the partnership between the endocrine and the autonomic nervous systems may be temporarily dissolved by the use of drugs that block the action of the sympathetic on the heart and allow a sufficient dose of thyroxine to be given. The heart muscle is gradually restored to health by thyroxine, while the excessive strain that would otherwise fall upon it by stimulation of the sympathetic is prevented by the adrenergic-blocking drug. For many years the thyroid was destroyed in seriously heart-sick patients by surgery or radioactive iodine, or restrained by the use of antithyroid drugs. The slow metabolism thus produced saved the flagging heart much work. Now such drastic measures have become unnecessary. The patient retains his thyroid intact but it is prevented from forcing the heart into an activity for which it has become unsuited.

The thyroid and the cardiovascular system are linked in other ways, of which the most obvious is the control of the peripheral blood vessels. The patient with too much thyroxine has a hot skin, the one with too little a cold skin. The temperature of the skin depends upon the blood flowing through it. Those who suffer from cold feet may feel that it is absurd that their extremities should lie so far away and so exposed to the weather. But there is method in this anatomical madness. The feet, and to a much smaller extent the hands and nose, have an important part to play in the regulation of body temperature. The skin (whatever its colour, racialists please note) is a most efficient radiator, especially in the long infra-red range, acting as a 'black body'. People whose metabolic rate is high and who therefore have more heat to lose have hot feet. There is indeed, other things being equal, an exact mathematical relationship between the basal metabolic rate and the toe temperature and therefore between thyroid activity and the toe temperature.

The adrenal cortex

The blood pressure is low in Addison's disease (adrenal deficiency) and high in Cushing's disease (adrenal excess) and when adrenal steroids are administered in excessive amounts to patients with rheumatoid arthritis and other diseases in which they have proved otherwise useful. The role played by the different cortical hormones in the regulation of blood pressure is not yet completely understood. The glucocorticoids are not very potent raisers of blood pressure, yet it is these that are present in excess both in Cushing's disease and in the over-treated rheumatic patient, conditions in which the blood pressure is high. Aldosterone is a very powerful raiser of blood pressure, but it does not seem to be present in excess in either of these states. When it is present in excess, as in the disease known as Conn's syndrome, there is no doubt of its potency and we know more of its mechanism. In Conn's syndrome the amount of potassium in the body is unduly low and that of sodium is high. When spironolactone, an antagonist to aldosterone, is given the levels of potassium and sodium return gradually to normal and, as they do so, the blood pressure subsides.

The adrenal medulla

The hormones of the adrenal medulla in healthy people and in ordinary circumstances have probably little importance in the control of blood pressure. Potentially, however, their influence is great, for the presence of adrenaline and noradrenaline, produced by the adrenal medulla in the proportion of about four to one, is correlated with the activity of the sympathetic, which in its turn, as we have seen, controls the rate of the heart beat and the calibre of the arteries. One of the greatest practical advances in medicine in recent years has been the discovery of various drugs that in various ways can block the activity of the sympathetic, lower the blood pressure, and, as we have seen in discussing the thyroid, slow the beating of the heart.

We do not see deficient medullary activity. Even when the adrenals have been destroyed by disease or removed by surgery a normal state may be maintained. Nevertheless, noradrenaline infused into the veins may be a life-saving measure when the blood pressure falls to dangerously low levels in surgical shock. An excessive production of the medullary hormones is, however, occasionally seen. A tumour of the adrenal medulla, known as a phaeochromocytoma, occurs and secretes excessive quantities of one hormone or the other or both. The excessive secretion occurs intermittently and causes attacks of sweating, pallor, trembling, headache, blurring of vision, pain in the chest and a high blood pressure which, though paroxysmal at first, eventually becomes sustained. All these symptoms can be controlled with drugs which antagonise the sympathetic and are permanently cured by removal of the tumour.

The gonadal hormones

Why is it that men, especially elderly ones, and elderly women, but rarely young ones, suffer from degeneration of their arteries and, in consequence, from heart attacks and strokes? At first sight one might guess (and one's guess would be as vague and inaccurate as most guesses are in medical science) that the oestrogens (secreted at a low level in men throughout life and in women after the menopause) protect our arteries, whereas testosterone from the testicles does the opposite. What is the more critical evidence for this?

First of all, testosterone, the secretion of the testicles, diminishes in men in old age and yet it is chiefly in old age, though not entirely, that old men become arteriosclerotic and suffer from coronary attacks.

The effects of testosterone have been carefully studied. Testosterone has a vasodilating action on the peripheral arteries. It causes, in humans, a lowering of blood pressure, an improvement in symptoms due to vasoconstriction, including such things as 'claudication', pain due to an insufficient supply of oxygen to the muscles of the legs called after the Emperor Claudius who limped. It has been claimed that it helps in angina pectoris, a condition known to be due to constriction of the coronary vessels supplying the heart muscle, but the evidence for this is suspect. Too many variables are involved – the degree to which the pain is due to additional effort, emotional effects, and the effects of cold. In human experiments there has been too little control of these variables and those physicians who have reported good results may well have infected their patients with undue optimism.

Yet there is no doubt that testosterone produces dilatation of the arteries. It also, by a central mechanism, has a 'tonic' action generally that might, apparently, improve results for the time being. Older men often feel 'better in themselves' under treatment with testosterone. The placebo reaction is one of which every doctor must be continuously aware when he is seeking to evaluate a drug. About thirty per cent of patients will feel better whatever treatment they are given. This is not necessarily a question of self-deception. We have already seen that a positive biochemical effect can be produced by emotional force. Thyrotoxicosis can undoubtedly be triggered off in this way, though perhaps only in predisposed individuals. It is a commonplace that diabetes mellitus may become much worse in conditions of emotional strain. Still more obvious to the ordinary observer is the fact that embarrassment may cause blushing, which is, after all, a dilatation of the blood vessels of the skin. Improvement under treatment by any means that induces optimism in the patient may be a very real thing.

Testosterone has been administered under carefully controlled conditions to castrated men, and it has been shown beyond peradventure to increase the blood supply, especially to the face, hands and feet. Spectrophotometric observations have shown an 'arterialisation' of the cutaneous blood – a change, that is, in the oxygen content of the veins. Ulceration in the skin due to a diminution in the supply of oxygen has been improved and walking ability has been increased.

Another fact is the effects of male and female hormones on the level of cholesterol in the blood, though the practical importance of this is still disputed. The administration of oestrogens reduces the level of cholesterol, whereas that of testosterone raises it. Unfortunately this effect of oestrogens cannot be achieved in men without feminisation, shown by reduction of libido and enlargement of the breasts. This may be a small price to pay if life is at stake, but this is still unsure. Certainly men who have undergone treatment with oestrogens because of carcinoma of the prostate have shown lowering of the blood cholesterol. Moreover, women whose ovaries have been removed in youth have an additional tendency to a high cholesterol level, and to the development of arterial degeneration and coronary disease of the heart. Nevertheless, the administration of oestrogens to those who have already developed coronary disease does not preclude a further heart attack.

In summary, we know that a high level of cholesterol in the blood is frequently associated with arterial degeneration generally and with coronary heart disease. We know of many things that lower the level, such as special diets, thyroid hormones and female sex hormones. We know that male hormones and certain diets tend to raise it. Yet we still do not know whether there is a cause and effect relationship between cholesterol levels and arterial disease or whether the artificial lowering of the cholesterol level in those in which it is abnormally high will do any good.

The parathyroid hormone

The action of the parathyroid hormone on the cardio-vascular system is not well defined. When parathormone is deficient, symptoms like those of angina have been described, presumably due to spasm of the coronary arteries. Raynaud's disease, in which the patient's fingers become white and cold, is sometimes seen. In severe cases, the electrocardiogram shows the specific changes of calcium deficiency, but there is no typical clinical syndrome. When parathormone is present in excess, calcium stones tend to be deposited in the kidneys and the disease of renal hypertension is common. Here again, the electrocardiogram displays a variety of changes from the normal pattern, but there is no characteristic clinical syndrome.

The pancreas

The complicated mechanism by which the blood sugar is maintained between narrow bounds fails in diabetes mellitus on the one hand and in hypoglycaemia on the other. It is not known how or why prolonged diabetes is associated with an increased tendency to arterial, and especially coronary, disease. Coronary disease occurs in sixty per cent of diabetics over fifty, men and women being equally affected. On the other hand of those who are not diabetics, only ten per cent suffer thus and the ratio of men to women is ten to one. The discovery of insulin has done much to reduce the incidence of cardiovascular complications in diabetes, but it has not stopped them. In fact the doctor today sees far more of these than his colleague a generation ago, for diabetics who would have died in the early years of this century are able to live long enough to experience the late results of this disease, coronary disease, strokes, gangrene of the toes, blindness and all the other manifestations of arteriosclerosis. In these patients the diabetes may always have been mild, even undetected. If patients with known coronary disease and apparently nothing else are studied by biochemical methods, a high proportion are found to be in fact diabetic.

The relationship between diabetes and arterial disease is one of the most fascinating mysteries of medicine. The two diseases tend to occur in the same families. In both there is a tendency to have a high level of cholesterol in the blood. On the other hand a normal level of cholesterol does not protect a diabetic from arterial complications, though it may be important that among diabetics in Ceylon both a high blood cholesterol and arteriosclerosis are uncommon.

Hypoglycaemia may be due to many things, including

overdosage with insulin, the presence of a secreting tumour of the islets of Langerhans of the pancreas, liver disease and emotional causes. As already explained, it produces an excessive release of adrenaline, the effect of which is to discharge glucose from the stores in the liver and restore a normal blood sugar. The cardiovascular effects of hypoglycaemia are due to adrenaline, the fast pulse and cold skin in particular.

14 Urology

The prostate

The prostate gland encircles the urethra of men below its exit from the bladder. Its function is the production of the fluid of the semen in which the spermatozoa swim. Enlargement in old age has been recognised from very early times and Sir Everard Home, now chiefly remembered for his destruction, after extensive cribbing, of his master John Hunter's manuscripts, believed that the words in Ecclesiastes, 'or the pitcher be broken at the fountain or the wheel broken at the cistern', referred to the uncontrolled micturition so common in 'the old man's disease'. Certainly enlargement of the prostate was recognised in the sixteenth century by Nicolo Massa and by Riolanus. John Hunter noticed in 1786 the difference between the prostates of whole men and eunuchs. Probably the first operations to relieve obstruction to the urinary flow were carried out by Blizzard in the early years of the nineteenth century.

The prostate is not a simple gland. Different parts of it are of different embryological origins, some 'male' and others 'female'. In man and in some but not all primates there exists a structure known as the uterus or utriculus masculinus that is of Müllerian and therefore 'female' origin. It is to be expected that such an organ would be responsive to female sex hormones and this has been found to be indeed so.

The uterus masculinus occupies the middle lobe of the prostate, the part of the gland in which senile benign enlargement begins.

The influence of hormones on the prostate has been suspected for a very long time. Eunuchs have very small prostates and the gland shrinks after castration. It was therefore quite natural that early workers in this field should have been led astray into thinking that spontaneous enlargement in later life must be due to an excessive production of male hormone. This false hypothesis led to castration as a method of treatment. Sometimes a temporary improvement resulted, for it did indeed produce a shrinking of the gland, but not of the diseased part, which continued to grow.

That it is not an excess of male hormone that produces the disease is suggested by several considerations. The gland of new-born infants is often enlarged, presumably by the action of the female hormones to which it is subject before birth. The output of male hormone from the testicles decreases even before the age at which enlargement usually occurs. Experimental exploration of this dilemma has been difficult because of the great differences that exist between the prostates of men and those of other animals. However, the administration of oestrogens to mice and rhesus monkeys is capable of producing histological changes very similar to those that occur spontaneously in man. These changes can be reversed by testosterone.

It seems that testosterone causes enlargement of the true gland. This is not a disease process but the physiological response of a target organ to its controlling hormone. Such an enlargement is common in dogs, but it causes them no inconvenience. However one dog has been described in which the prostate was histologically abnormal and very like a diseased human gland. Moreover this dog exhibited several feminine characteristics that suggested the excessive production of an oestrogen.

Oestrogens do not cause enlargement of the prostate itself but of the 'female' component, the uterus masculinus in the middle lobe. Castration and oestrogenic treatment may produce a temporary improvement by causing shrinkage of

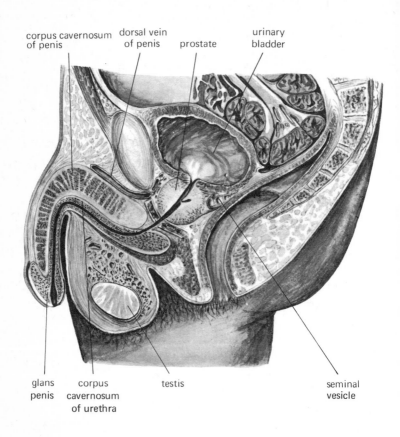

corpus cavernosum of penis   dorsal vein of penis   prostate   urinary bladder

glans penis   corpus cavernosum of urethra   testis   seminal vesicle

the gland as a whole, but enlargement of the uterus masculinus continues, perhaps even faster, and gradually overtakes any improvement that may have occurred. Although many reports of dramatic cures by means of oestrogens have been reported, it is remarkable that prolonged 'follow ups' have not been published.

It would seem then that the problem has been solved, but this is far from the truth. For many years doctors in many countries have attempted to treat benign enlargement of the prostate by means of male hormones, and brilliant results have been claimed. It is remarkable how large a number of workers have published just one paper on their results and have then retired into an uneasy silence. Probably some of these papers were premature, the benefits later turning out to be temporary. Testosterone has a remarkable tonic effect on the bladder muscles, sufficient often to overcome lesser degrees of urethral obstruction of whatever cause, even in women.

The failure of treatment with testosterone may be due simply to the fact that the change produced by oestrogens is not reversible. It is likely too that this simple hypothesis is too simple, other hormones being involved. Further research in this field is overdue. Perhaps the good results of modern surgery have dulled the interest of research workers or have deflected their interest on to diseases less easily curable by such means.

One of these is cancer of the prostate, the cause of death in about five per cent of men over fifty years of age. The root cause of the cancer is as obscure as that of cancer anywhere else: it is possibly not endocrine at all. The importance of hormones in this disease lies in the fact that androgens make it worse and oestrogens make it better. This might be expected from the fact that the disease arises predominantly in the true gland, not in the uterus masculinus. Unfortunately cancer of the prostate is all too often diagnosed when it is too advanced for treatment by surgery and radio-therapy to be more than palliative. There remains the modification of the endocrine environment, the results of which are encouraging.

The adverse activity of testosterone may be reduced by castration, which produces a remarkable improvement in a few days, but doubt still exists as to whether this psychologically traumatic treatment produces results any better than the use of oestrogens. These act by suppressing the output of chorionic gonadotrophin from the pituitary, without which the testicles cease to produce testosterone. Their side-effects, impotence and the swelling of the male breasts, are a small price for an elderly man to pay for the prolongation of a life he may still enjoy. Unfortunately, we must still speak of prolongation of life rather than of cure.

Kidney stones

Endocrine influences on the urinary tract are discernible in the production of 'stones' in the kidney. The exact way in which these deposits of calcium come about is still not known. We know however that their presence is one of the most common signals of the presence of tumours of the parathyroid glands.

Stones in the kidneys are of many kinds but it is only in the calcium containing ones that the endocrine system has at present been inculpated. Probably various factors are involved, such as inadequate drainage, insufficient drinking of fluids, foreign bodies in the urinary tract, errors in diet, and infection. Excessive production of parathyroid hormones causes, as we have seen, a high level of calcium in the blood. In some instances, the kidneys are unable to excrete the excess and the calcium is retained within them. That some patients with parathyroid tumours do not form stones is obviously due to the necessity for some other factor to act in partnership with the excessive passage of calcium through the kidneys.

Water balance

One of the most fascinating of the integrative actions of the endocrine glands lies in the control of the kidneys by the posterior lobe of the pituitary gland. In diabetes insipidus, a lesion of the hypothalamus or of the tract leading to the posterior pituitary or of the posterior pituitary itself suppresses the production of antidiuretic hormone, the function of which is to cause the tubules of the kidney to reabsorb water. The brilliant work of Verney and his associates was done on dogs but they are of undoubted human significance. They showed that dogs in an anxious state secrete an excess of the hormone vasopressin and thus increase the retention of water in the tissues, and explained in quantitative terms the century-old observation of Claude Bernard that anxiety and fear cause waterlogging of the body. Emotional fluid retention was often seen during the war. Examples are given on page 245.

The pituitary is not alone in its control of the water balance. The adrenal participates, partly by the effect of cortisol already described but chiefly by the secretion of aldosterone, which controls the reabsorption of sodium in the renal tubules. The secretion of aldosterone is itself controlled by the renin-angiotism mechanism (see chapter 11). Renin, produced in the kidney, reacts with a protein in the blood to produce angiotensin and this stimulates the adrenal cortex to increase its output of aldosterone. The question is, of course, what controls the level of renin production. One stimulus is reduced plasma volume such as occurs in severe haemorrhage, but there are probably others. A much neglected clinical fact is that a majority of women suffering from obesity have demonstrable swelling along their shins. Whether this is of hypothalamic origin is unknown.

Diabetes mellitus

No account of the relationship of the endocrine system and the kidneys would be complete without mention of the fact that many diabetics die from kidney failure. The mechanism is not completely understood. We know that the proteins and electrolytes in the blood are disturbed, that the level of cholesterol is high, that the adrenals produce more cortisol and less male hormone, and that there is a deficiency of vitamin B12, all in addition to the changes to be expected from a deficiency of insulin or antagonism to its action. It seems not unlikely that an abnormality of the adrenals is present, for this would explain many but not all of the abnormalities found.

In only one digestive trouble has any one of the numerous digestive hormones been inculpated. In this single instance, known as the Zollinger-Ellison syndrome, intractable diarrhoea and repeated and multiple ulcers of the small intestine have been found to be associated with a tumour of the pancreas, an excessive secretion of gastrin, and a very high gastric acidity. However secretin, gastrin and pancreozymin all, when given by mouth, have an action in stimulating the secretion of insulin and pancreozymin stimulates also that of glucagon. These facts may be involved in the still mysterious origins of diabetes mellitus. In the type that occurs in later life secretin does indeed cause a fall in blood sugar.

More common in these days of the often excessive use of cortisone is the gastric or duodenal ulceration that sometimes occurs when the hormone is administered in excessive amounts for too long a period. We have seen that cortisol, the natural form of the hormone, is secreted in excess in conditions of stress as a part of the protective reaction of the body, and ulcers sometimes occur after severe burns, frostbite, coronary attacks, surgical operations, psychological shock or severe illness of many kinds. The ulcers may cause profuse haemorrhage and even death. They sometimes occur in Cushing's disease in which there is an abnormal secretion of cortisol.

Many experiments have been made in an attempt to explain the action of adrenal steroids on the lining of the stomach and intestines. One thing is sure: it is not local irritation that causes the trouble, as it is with aspirin. We know that after removal of the pituitary, which of course causes depression of the adrenals, and in Addison's disease, there is a fall in the acidity of gastric juice and it might be inferred that in the opposite sets of conditions there might be excessive acidity. In Simmonds' disease and Addison's disease the gastric acidity is restored by treatment with cortisone. The effects of such treatment vary greatly from one animal to another, which makes experiment difficult. In men the effects are very variable. Could it be that those who respond by an increase in gastric juice and in its acidity when treated with cortisone are those more liable to develop ulcers in times of stress? This point does not seem to have been considered. That it is the whole answer is unlikely, for ulcers are sometimes seen in patients with no acid in their stomachs. Long ago, too, Selye dropped a large spanner into the works by showing that stress produced more ulcers in rats without their adrenals, and that adequate substitution therapy protected them. As so often, our increase in knowledge is bedevilled by species differences. Rats and men, so much alike in some respects, are very unlike in others. They are alike in one respect that may be important: in both, the healing of skin wounds is retarded by treatment with adrenal steroids. It seems likely that the adrenal steroids cause ulceration in man's stomach and small intestine by retarding the healing of abrasions.

When one thinks about that extremely common disease of modern times, the chronic gastric and duodenal ulcer, one is surprised not by its frequency but by its relative infrequency. The lining of the stomach and duodenum must be subjected to almost as many hazards as the skin of the hands, and is far more fragile. Hard food insufficiently chewed and bits of sharp bone are probably swallowed daily by almost all of us. The healing capacity of the mucous membrane must be amazingly efficient. Maybe the difference between the ulcer patient and the man with a cast iron digestion lies in this healing capacity, interfered with in some by an excess of acid gastric juice, in others by deficient mucus and in others by variations in the adrenal response to stress or even by the sensitivity of the target organ, the mucous membrane of the stomach and small intestine, to the adrenal hormones.

It certainly seems that the occurrence of peptic ulcers is not necessarily dependent on a high level in the blood of adrenal steroids. Other factors must be involved. Nevertheless, the presence in excess of these hormones is undoubtedly a factor to be considered when there is undue stress of any kind, psychological or otherwise, and when treatment with these hormones is given in rheumatoid arthritis or in other conditions in which such treatment may be necessary to health or even to life.

The thyroid may also be involved in the health of the stomach. This will be discussed in the chapter devoted to the influence of the endocrine system on diseases of the blood. It is interesting to recall that in hyperthyroidism, a condition associated clinically with continuous psychological stress, stomach ulcers do not occur with undue frequency although gastritis is common. This may be related to the fact that hyperthyroid patients tend to have less acid in their stomachs, apparently because a large proportion of them harbour an 'antigastric antibody'. This is even more true of patients with Hashimoto's disease, now accepted as an autoimmune disease (see chapter 22). Many cases of hyperthyroidism are reasonably regarded as due to this mechanism.

There are other rare and curious relationships between hormones and the digestive tract. An excessive secretion of parathyroid hormone is usually thought of in connection with stones in the kidney and brittle bones. It has been called a disease of stones, bones and abdominal groans. It is commonly accompanied by loss of appetite, nausea, vomiting, constipation and pain in the upper part of the abdomen and even ulceration, and similar symptoms occur during the over-energetic treatment of those unfortunate patients whose parathyroid glands have been inadvertently removed during operations on the adjoining thyroid. Some of the patients who develop these symptoms spontaneously are found to have tumours not only in the parathyroids but in the pancreas and are suffering from the Zollinger-Ellison syndrome, but the question is complicated by the fact that in patients with parathyroid tumours the level of calcium in the blood is unduly high and that similar symptoms may be seen when this is raised by an entirely different mechanism. It has recently been found by post-mortem studies that most patients with chronic duodenal and gastric ulcers have enlarged parathyroid glands whereas those with acute ulcers have not. This suggests that the action of the parathyroids is not to cause ulcers but to prevent their healing. It may be that the high level of calcium they produce in the blood causes an increase in gastric acidity. Again this cannot be the sole cause because of the not infrequent occurrence of ulcers in the presence of a normal or even subnormal acidity.

One of the most unpleasant and ultimately fatal diseases of the digestive tract is ulcerative colitis, a disease of unknown origin that produces continuous diarrhoea and the discharge of blood and mucus from the rectum. Treatment with cortisone applied by means of an enema is effective but not curative. The best that can be said is that a temporary improvement is obtained in a high proportion of patients. Temporary improvement may also be seen in steatorrhoea, a condition in which the patient is unable to absorb fat. How cortisone works in either of these conditions is unknown.

The liver, though itself a gland and the main chemical

laboratory of the body, is subject to endocrine influence from many quarters. It is the organ in which many hormones, as well as other substances, are detoxicated, rendered harmless, and converted into the form in which they are excreted by the kidneys. One of these is oestradiol. If the liver fails to deactivate oestradiol it accumulates in the blood in an active form. Even men produce a little of this fundamentally female hormone and its accumulation may cause enlargement of the breasts, loss of pubic and axillary hair, and atrophy of the testicles. In women the excess of circulating oestrogen may cause excessive uterine bleeding. The activity of the liver may be impaired by cirrhosis, as in alcoholics, by poisons such as carbon tetrachloride, a common constituent of cleaning fluids, or by vitamin deficiencies.

The importance of the liver in carbohydrate metabolism is discussed in chapter 8.

16 Respiration

The respiratory tract begins at the nostrils and extends through the nose, pharynx, larynx, trachea and bronchi to the ultimate air sacks or alveoli. No part of it can claim exemption from endocrine control.

This is not surprising for in the embryo the primitive mouth or stomodaeum is formed by the invagination of the epiblast. From its top Rathke's pouch grows upwards between the pre-sphenoidal and post-sphenoidal centres of ossification to meet, at the fourth week, another pouch descending from the third ventricle of the brain, thus to form the pituitary gland.

There are numerous occasions on which the interests of laryngology and endocrinology overlap. There is, for instance, for the surgeon the nasal approach to the pituitary. The growth of the larynx is under control by the sex hormones, which accounts for its larger size in the male and his deeper voice. The most important common ground in the upper respiratory tract is the growth of the skull and the health of the mucous membranes.

We see the effects of the anterior pituitary most clearly in gigantism, acromegaly and pituitary dwarfism. In gigantism the α or eosinophil cells of the pituitary produce an excessive amount of growth hormone during the normal period of growth. For the most part the correct relative proportions are maintained except that owing to the powerful effect of the hormone on cartilage the limbs tend to be disproportionately long. Sometimes in the skull the normal changes of maturation are exaggerated. The maxilla of a child consists of little more that the alveolus and the frontal process. As age advances the antrum develops and the vertical height increases, changes that are sometimes exaggerated in the giant so that a typical facial form emerges. Acromegaly, occurring as we have

16·1 The development of the pituitary gland. The figures show how the infundibular process grows down from the brain to form the posterior pituitary while the pharynx grows up to the anterior pituitary.

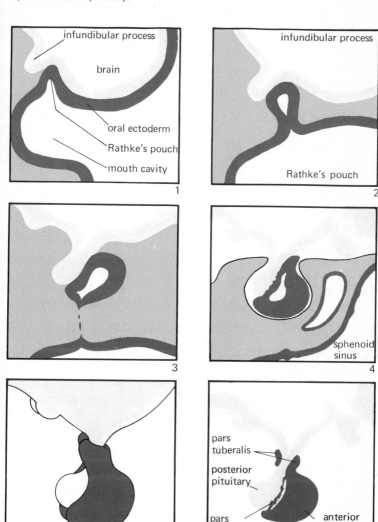

seen when normal growth has ceased, cannot affect the bones produced in cartilage. Instead soft tissues and bones developed from membrane undergo excessive growth. The sinuses are unduly large and the facial tissues coarse and ribbed like those of a blood-hound. Enlargement of the larynx produces a remarkably deep voice. The uvula, soft palate, turbinals and nasal mucous membrane are thickened so that the nasal passages, unduly roomy though they are, become obstructed. On the contrary, in pituitary deficiency underdevelopment of the face and sinus maintain a child-like visage. The accompanying thyroid deficiency causes premature union of the parts of the sphenoid bone resulting in the broad depressed nasal bridge of the cretin. The accompanying gonadal deficiency causes deficient growth of the larynx and the high voice of the eunuch.

The relationship between sexual function and the mucous membrane of the nose is said to have been known to Hippocrates. As long ago as 1884 Mackenzie observed that the nasal mucosa of women becomes congested before the menstrual periods. Some women tend to suffer from a running nose and asthma at this time. In monkeys there is an increase in colour of the nasal mucosa at monthly intervals coincident with the swelling of the sexual skin. Monkeys of both sexes, whether intact or castrated, react to treatment with oestrogens by reddening of the mucous membrane, even if it is transplanted elsewhere. Conversely the disease of atrophic rhinitis, in which the nasal mucous membrane is thin and pale, can often be relieved by the instillation of an oestrogen, which produces vasodilatation and regeneration.

The action of adrenaline on the nasal congestion of hay fever is known to all the numerous sufferers from this distressing complaint. Here its activity is solely that of a decongestant. Its action on the bronchi is more complex. Some asthmatic patients develop attacks in moments of stress, when it may be presumed that adrenaline is plentiful and it has been shown experimentally that in some circumstances it may have a constricting effect on the bronchi. It remains, however, a remedy on which many asthmatics have come to rely implicitly.

The use of adrenal corticoids in hay fever and asthma rests upon the anti-allergic and anti-inflammatory properties of cortisol and similar drugs. In the former, a steroid snuff affords dramatic temporary relief, though one wonders, in these days of highly successful desensitisation, why such treatment should be necessary. Asthma far less regularly responds to densensitisation. This may be due in part to the chronic infection that so often supervenes in older patients, the bacterial invasion swamping the original allergic cause. Even in younger patients it may be difficult or impossible to find the responsible allergen, the usual skin tests so often showing sensitivity to everything or nothing. Moreover in many patients a strong psychological element is present, though it is improbable that asthma is ever of purely psychological origin.

Earlier reports on the use of cortisone and cortisol in asthma were far from encouraging. Carefully conducted trials provided little support for their use and plenty of support for those who feared their side effects. The longer one has used adrenal steroids (and the author has done so since 1946, before the popularisation of the 'wonder drug' in America) the more cautious one becomes. The old adage *curare cito, tuto et jucunde* is out of fashion today, the necessity for safety, *tuto*, being often forgotten. Nevertheless, just as a good play slammed by the critics may run for years because the gallery likes it, the steroids in the treatment of asthma have refused to leave the stage. There is now no doubt that in status asthmaticus, a condition in which severe asthma continues despite old and well-tried treatments and threatens the life of the patient, cortisone and other steroids are life-saving. In chronic asthma the result of steroid therapy is less dramatic but, in the absence of bronchitis, often beneficial. Nevertheless, of every patient the question must be asked, Which is more dangerous, the treatment or the disease?

Corticosteroids have been found to be of great value in the treatment of many diseases of the eyes, largely because of their suppressive action on inflammatory processes. The body has a decided tendency to panic and overdo its own defence and it sometimes happens that the defenders of the city do more harm than the attackers. The special value of corticosteroids in ocular disease lies in the fact that they can be used locally and are not absorbed in sufficient quantity to bring about the disastrous side-effects so commonly seen when they are given by mouth or by injection. Among these are the swelling of the conjunctivae and haemorrhages, which are so often seen in patients overtreated with steroids for such diseases as rheumatoid arthritis and in naturally occurring Cushing's disease. Glaucoma (raised intraocular pressure) and opacities of the lens have occasionally been seen even during local treatment too enthusiastically applied. The intraocular pressure is especially liable to rise in patients belonging to families in which glaucoma is common. Diabetes mellitus tends to occur in the same families and it may be that similar genes are involved.

Diabetes is a frequent cause of blindness, accounting for ten per cent of blindness in the United States. It causes progressive degeneration of the retina, visible in a large proportion of diabetics who have had the disease for over ten years. Unfortunately careful control of the diabetes by diet and insulin does little or nothing to arrest the progress of the retinal part of the disease. Happily there is some hope that its progress may be stopped by removal or destruction of the pituitary gland or cutting of the pituitary stalk. Simmonds' disease, fairly easily controlled by hormone therapy, is a small price to pay for the prevention of total blindness. The role of the pituitary in diabetic retinitis is not completely

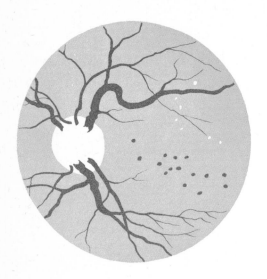

17·1 The fundus of the eye in diabetes mellitus. The white spots are exudates and the red ones haemorrhages into the retina.

understood and the discovery of the beneficial result of pituitary destruction was accidental. It is likely that the factor responsible is the growth hormone.

Cataracts, opacities in the lens of the eye, are another common complication of diabetes mellitus, happily one that can be dealt with by surgery. The ocular complications of diabetes are numerous and in this book their enumeration would be inappropriate.

Other endocrine conditions are related to the eyes. Pituitary tumours by pressing on the optic nerves may cause reduction in the visual fields. In deficiency of the parathyroid glands cataract is common. But perhaps the most interesting ocular changes are those that occur in thyroid disease.

The protruding eyes of patients with overactivity of the thyroid gland, and occasionally also when it is deficient in activity, are dramatic enough to make the diagnosis obvious to the man in the street, and obscure enough to be of interest to the specialist.

The connective tissues of the body consist of cells, fibres and the ground substance that lies between them. The ground substance consists of complexes of carbohydrate and protein: the mucopolysaccharides, which are largely carbohydrate, and the glycoproteins, which are largely protein – the two occurring in different combinations in different sites. The synthesis of these substances is brought about by enzymes that are affected in their activity by hormones. An example of this is the deposit of mucopolysaccharide in the skin of patients deficient in thyroid activity. It produces the coarse pale swollen look of so-called myxoedema seen in patients with profound thyroid deficiency. Because it is deposited in the larynx, the voice is thick and hoarse, and in the heart it may cause heart failure. In the skin it sometimes produces the unsightly swelling of the legs called local myxoedema. In the eyes it causes the protrusion known as exophthalmos. In mild cases, the substance deposited behind the eyes that pushes them forward is mostly fat and fluid, but in severe cases it consists of mucopolysaccharide. The exact part played by thyroxine and thyrotrophin has not been elucidated. LATS, the long-acting thyroid stimulator, is not responsible. It may even be that another substance altogether, called mesenchymotrophic hormone or the exophthalmos-producing substance, may be involved.

Thyroid exophthalmos is, when severe, associated with paralysis of one or more of the muscles of the eye, with gross swelling or inflammation of the conjuctiva and occasional

17·2 Below left Malignant exophthalmos persisting after the cure of Graves' disease. Protrusion of the eyes and oedema of the lids have persisted, though the upper lid retraction has given place to drooping of the upper lids.
17·3 Below right In this case of Graves' disease, the upper lids have retracted to expose the white sclera above the iris, but there is no exophthalmos. There is paralysis of the upward movement of the left eye.

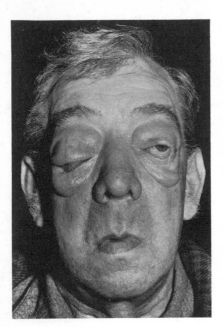 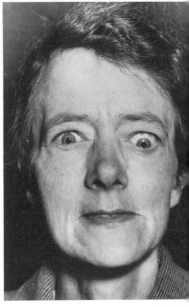

atrophy of the optic nerves. Happily it usually improves slowly over the years when the underlying thyroid disease has been cured, but occasionally surgery may be called for to save the sight.

We do not understand the cause of exophthalmos, but another condition, often confused with it, is a spasm of the eyelids that is well understood. It produces a stare that may closely imitate the appearance of true protrusion. This is due to the stimulant action of excessive thyroxine on the sympathetic nervous system, which controls the action of the muscles of the upper eyelids. Upper lid retraction produced

17·4 Below left Malignant exophthalmos of Graves' disease. Note the engorgement of the blood vessels of the eyeball.

17·5 Below right Another case of severe exophthalmos in Graves' disease.

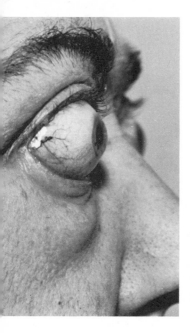

in this way is unsightly but harmless. Unlike exophthalmos, it is rapidly relieved by treatment of the underlying hyperthyroidism. It is also relieved by drugs that block the action of the sympathetic nervous system.

18 The skin

The whole picture of dermatology has changed since the introduction of cortisone. Corticoids of this type, locally applied, are now used in a large number of skin diseases. We still know little of why they work: the point is that they do.

The skin is not merely an integument or cloak. It is the largest organ in the body and one of the most important. In the average man it measures 1·85 square metres and its weight is about sixteen per cent of the total weight of the body, averaging 4·8 kilograms. It is an important radiator helping to maintain the correct temperature of the body both by variations in its blood supply and by the production of sweat. When the body temperature is too high the blood supply is increased and more heat is radiated, sweating is increased and more heat is lost by evaporation. Too low a body temperature is countered by vasoconstriction and therefore less radiation and by a reduction of sweat and evaporation. Both processes are under combined autonomic and endocrine control. In hyperthyroidism increased oxidation generates heat so that the blood vessels dilate and the sweat glands pour out their secretion. In hypothyroidism, contraction of the vessels and diminution of sweat produce the cold dry skin of the patient with myxoedema. Even in our temperate zone, many old and lonely people die every winter from a combination of thyroid deficiency and a cold environment.

Sweat glands

These are of two kinds. The ordinary yellow ones, called eccrine, are distributed over the whole body and are present before birth. They are coiled tubular structures and their total length amounts to about eight miles. They produce an odourless sweat. Their main function is the control of body temperature through evaporation, but they also excrete salts under the influence of the adrenal cortex. The other kind of sweat gland, called apocrine, begins to function only at puberty. Apocrine glands are red, and are found chiefly in the armpits, on the mons veneris and around the anus and the nipples. They produce the sweat that is responsible for the characteristic odour of the body, by some considered sexually attractive but by others repulsive, and popularly known as BO. The apocrine glands are of great commercial importance. Were it not for them the town of Grasse would have little significance.

Sebaceous glands

The skin also carries the sebaceous glands that produce the natural oil of the skin, the main function of which is to maintain a soft skin texture and prevent undue drying. Their secretion, called sebum, begins in childhood but is greatly increased at puberty. Their activity is increased by testosterone and reduced by castration and by the administration of oestrogens. The sudden increase in their activity at puberty often results in traffic congestion in their ducts which become plugged by thickened sebum. This easily becomes infected by the micro-organisms always present on the skin. Acne, the curse of adolescents, then occurs. This disease was known in remote antiquity.

The origin of the name is obscure. It was first used by one Aetius who was physician to Justinian the Great in the sixth century AD. Since the seventeenth century the relationship between acne and sexual function has been recognised but sometimes misunderstood. Thus Jonston of Amsterdam in 1648 believed that it occurs in 'young people that are inclined to venery and fruitful but chast withal and continent'. The association between acne and the menstrual cycle was early realised. That acne tends to occur especially in those who practise masturbation was an idea long prevalent among schoolmasters: the fact that acne is not universal passed unnoticed. Eunuchs do not suffer from acne. Women with virilising tumours of the adrenals or ovaries do so. A useful early sign of overdosage of hormones given to increase the growth of undergrown children is the appearance of a spotty face. Oestrogens have the opposite effect. The occurrence of acne in women in the days before menstruation is common but its cause is unknown.

Hair

The hair is derived almost exclusively from the epidermis, the surface layer of the skin. It is not a permanent structure. Mature hairs are shed at the rate of about a hundred a day from the human scalp, which in this respect resembles an evergreen tree. The relationship between hormones and hair growth is obvious: pubic and axillary hair first occur at puberty; men and women have a different distribution of hair; a female distribution can be induced in men by large doses of oestrogen; a male distribution is seen in women with androgen-producing tumours of the adrenals. In both sexes pituitary deficiency with its accompanying gonadal and adrenal deficiency results in general hairlessness. Amongst the most frequent disorders seen in an endocrine clinic are baldness and excessive hair in women.

Baldness occurs in several forms. Frontal baldness in women is often due to adrenal overactivity and is usually associated with an excessive growth of hair elsewhere

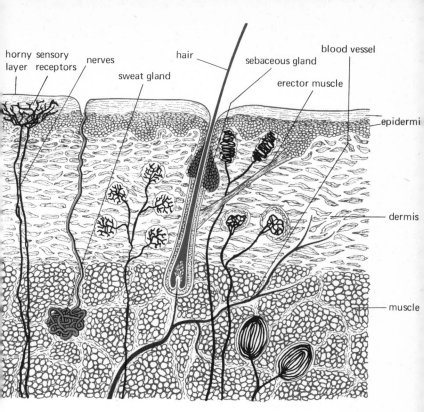

horny layer sensory receptors nerves sweat gland hair sebaceous gland erector muscle blood vessel epidermis dermis muscle

Unfortunately when hair has ceased to grow for several years the removal of the original cause may not be followed by regrowth. Conversely the hair may continue to grow excessively elsewhere. The reason for this is not known: it looks like habit. This is most obvious in the beard of the elderly man which may actually grow more profusely despite a drop in testicular function. When excessive growth of the beard occurs in women as a result of excessive adrenal function the removal of the adrenals may have little or no effect upon it. But though the testicular secretion undoubtedly increases the hair growth over all other parts of the body, it seems to have the opposite effect on the scalp. Frontal baldness is a masculine characteristic and in ancient times it was known as

18·2 Left Androgen-producing tumour of the right adrenal gland. The tumour was benign but its massive production of androgen over the years caused the woman to become more masculine in appearance. She had to shave twice a day and developed frontal baldness. The breasts atrophied, menstruation ceased, and the clitoris enlarged.

18·3 Right St Wilgefort, an effigy in Westminster Abbey. To a similar effigy in St Paul's Cathedral, wives offered oats in the hope that she would rid them of their husbands. She was a princess of Portugal, about to be married to a suitor she did not love. She prayed to be made unattractive to him and her prayer was answered, presumably by causing her to develop an adrenal tumour. She devoted her life to religion and, not surprisingly, died a virgin.

'noble baldness' and was ascribed to the pressure of the martial helmet. A woman with an adrenal tumour may develop severe frontal baldness which, because of this mysterious 'habit' of hair growth, may remain when the tumour has been removed. A woman treated with testosterone for, for instance, cancer of the breast, develops hair on the face that may persist when treatment is withdrawn. Nevertheless, treatment of a man with an oestrogen for, for instance, cancer of the prostate, slows the growth of the beard and pubic hair. It may entirely cease in those rare instances when a psychologically unbalanced man treats himself with excessive amounts of oestrogen in order to ape the appearance of femininity. In such cases frontal baldness may disappear. Indeed, in endocrine disturbance, natural or induced, the behaviour of the hair is strangely unpredictable.

Excessive hair growth in women otherwise normally feminine is an important medical problem that causes much unhappiness and even suicide. All such cases must be

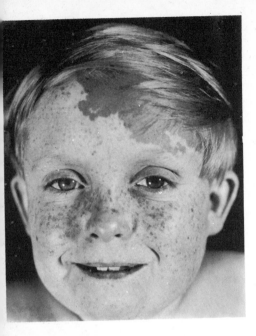

18·4 Left Vitiligo in a pituitary dwarf. Patchy pigmentation of this kind is rather common in a variety of endocrine disorders, especially in Graves' disease and Addison's disease. The reason for this is unknown.

18·5 Right Addison's disease. Two patients with general pigmentation of the skin. In this condition the failure of the adrenal cortex to produce cortisol has led to an excessive production of pituitary corticotrophin and perhaps of melanotrophic hormone.

investigated carefully lest a tumour or adrenal overactivity may be present. In others, such as the Stein-Leventhal syndrome to be mentioned again later, the androgen producing the excessive hair may be of ovarian origin. In the majority, especially of the less severe cases, no definite abnormality of either gland can be proven. Some cases of excessive hair growth are undoubtedly of genetic origin. It is normal for women of Mediterranean stock to carry more hair than their Nordic sisters. The remainder are often explained by 'target organ sensitivity', it being assumed that the hair follicles are unduly sensitive to a normal androgenic stimulus. It must be remembered that all normal men have some oestrogen in their blood, secreted by both adrenals and gonads and that all women carry some androgen with similar origins. Moreover, there is a spectrum of hair growth between the two extremes of masculinity and femininity, not a sharp division. A hand lens can detect slight hair growth on the face of the most

feminine Nordic blonde, so much so that many film actresses must use a depilatory wax lest the violent light of the studio should expose it. Just as a woman may have a large, medium or small nose, so may she have a growth of facial hair varying from the obviously excessive to the undetectable. Nevertheless, evidence is accumulating that many women thus afflicted have minor abnormalities of adrenal secretion, presumably due to slight abnormalities of their adrenal enzymes. Some, too, seem to have adrenals that react too violently to stimulation with corticotrophin, so that in all conditions of stress, psychological or physical, the adrenals tend to excrete an excessive amount not only of the cortisol demanded by the circumstances but of androgen as well. Here, too, genetics may enter into the picture, for many hirsute women with no demonstrable disease of adrenals or ovaries have broad shoulders and narrow hips.

The control of excessive hair growth in women has not been

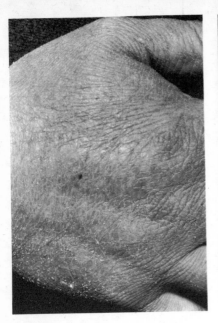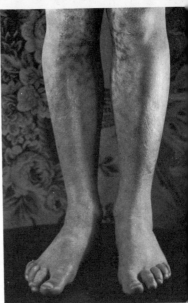

achieved, though ointments containing a high proportion of oestrogen applied after depilation with wax have had a limited success in occasional cases. Usually these unfortunate women must rely on cosmetic measures such as plucking, waxing, electrolysis and the use of depilatories. The simplest treatment is by shaving, which does not encourage its growth.

Frontal baldness may, then, be a sign of a high production of androgens but another form is more mysterious, the patchy type know as alopecia areata that may recover spontaneously or spread to involve the whole body, when it is known as alopecia universalis. Its cause is still unknown. It responds however to treatment with adrenal steroids. When these are injected into the affected areas hair grows again, but the growth is patchy and cosmetically far from satisfactory. When cortisone or another adrenal steroid is given by mouth the effect is very satisfactory. Hair grows again, but only while treatment is continued. Continued treatment with these hormones is a hazardous procedure, involving the risk of diabetes mellitus, duodenal ulcer, spontaneous bleeding into the skin and a rise in blood pressure. A wig seems preferable, especially today when many women wear wigs at the dictate of fashion.

Alopecia diffusa, a condition in which the hair of the scalp becomes generally scanty but without actual baldness is not as a rule of endocrine origin. It may be caused by infection, a variety of drugs, by mental shock or stress or by iron deficiency, and occasionally by thyroid deficiency, of which it may be the only obvious sign. Curiously enough it may also occur when the thyroid activity is excessive.

Pigmentation

In the epidermis lie the melanocytes, the cells that harbour the granules of the black pigment melanin that determines the difference between the black and white races and between the blonde and the brunette. In the skin of the albino there are no melanocytes. In that of the negro and the sunbather, who with a laudable absence of racial prejudice attempts to achieve a similar degree of pigmentation, they are numerous, for ultraviolet light encourages the production of melanin. They are also numerous in Addison's disease (adrenal gland deficiency) and in certain other endocrine disorders.

The number of the melanocytes and their content of pigment are both under the control of the pituitary hormone known sometimes as intermedin (because in some animals it is produced in a lobe intermediate between the anterior and posterior parts of the pituitary), and sometimes as the melanocyte-stimulating hormone, or MSH for short. In several conditions in which the pituitary produces an excessive amount of corticotrophin, extra MSH is also produced.

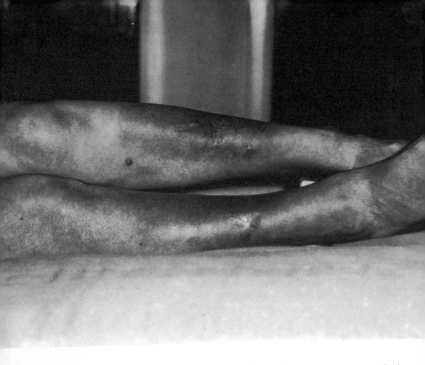

Indeed at one time it was argued that they were one and the same hormone. However they have definite chemical differences, though it is still regarded as possible that corticotrophin may have an effect of its own on pigmentation. In Addison's disease, in which the feed-back action of the adrenal cortex ceases to operate, and after surgical removal of the adrenals because of Cushing's disease, in which the cortex is overacting, there is an increased output of MSH and the skin darkens, often to an almost negroid extent. The darkening may be prevented by the administration of a corticoid such as cortisone. However, MSH is not the only hormone involved in pigmentation. Testosterone seems to be necessary for the production of a successful suntan. Castrates do not tan and the histochemical examination of their skin shows a low content of melanin. Ovarian hormones cause increased pigmentation of the nipples and the female genitalia. A patchy pigmentation of the face, especially

18 8 Cushing's syndrome.
Protein deficiency has reduced
the elastic tissue of the body,
causing spontaneous bleeding
into the skin and undue susceptibility
to minor injury.

201

around the mouth and eyes, is common in pregnancy and may be due to the combined effect of oestrogens and pro-gestogens, the levels of both of which are then high. A variation in facial pigmentation has been observed during the menstrual cycle, the skin becoming darker in some women before menstruation when both ovarian hormones are at their zenith in the blood. In Simmonds' disease, in which the pituitary has been destroyed, pigmentation cannot be induced by sunshine, but whether this is due to a lack of MSH or of testosterone or of oestradiol or of all of them is still un-known. The action of the sex hormones is probably to make the skin more sensitive to MSH. It must not be forgotten that disorders of pigmentation may occur in an immense variety of skin diseases, in vitamin deficiencies and as a result of drugs, and that these are not known to be related to endo-crine disorders.

Connective tissue

Connective tissue, present in every organ of the body, consists of cells, fibres, and intercellular ground substance. The last consist of combinations of protein and carbo-hydrate. As we saw in the last chapter, when protein is predominant the complex is known as a glycoprotein; when carbohydrate is predominant it is called a mucopolysac-charide. Quite a lot is known about the latter and several have been characterised, the best known being hyaluronic acid, chondroitin sulphate and keratosulphate. These are distributed in different proportions in different organs, the ground substance of the skin containing mainly hyaluronic acid and chondroitin sulphate. Several hormones, by altering the activities of enzymes necessary to the metabolism of these substances, produce changes in the skin.

This is well seen in the case of hypothyroidism, in which there is an accumulation of mucopolysaccharide in the skin, which becomes thickened by it. Other organs are similarly affected, but it is with the skin that we are here concerned. It appears that for the full development of myxoedema and its characteristic pale coarse skin both a low thyroid activity and a high secretion of thyrotrophin by the pituitary are necessary, the two acting in different ways. When the thyroid deficiency is due to pituitary deficiency there is a slight increase in ground substance but the typical appearance of myxoedema is not seen. It is possible that the swelling of the legs called pretibial myxoedema seen in occasional patients with disordered thyroids is due to too much thyrotrophin with normal or high thyroxine, but the place of the long-acting thyroid stimulator is probably important also.

The effects of the adrenal steroids on ground substance are being extensively explored. Cortisol and similar hormones reduce the formation of hyaluronic acid and therefore of ground substance; connective tissue is weakened. The effects are similar to those of age. In patients with Cushing's disease, bleeding occurs in the skin from small vessels unsupported by connective tissue. In this condition, the surface layers of the skin are curiously fragile, a mere stroke being enough to tear away a whole area from the deeper tissues. Similar changes in the skin are all too often seen in patients treated with cortisone with unwise enthusiasm.

The skin mirrors the health of the whole body and in particular it reflects the endocrine state with remarkable perspicacity.

It has already been seen in earlier chapters that the volume and constitution of the blood are controlled to an important extent by the ductless glands.

Blood volume

The hormones of the kidney are primarily responsible for the volume of the blood. It seems that the secretion of aldosterone by the adrenals is largely controlled by the reninangiotensin system of the kidneys (chapter 11) and aldosterone controls the levels of sodium and potassium, themselves immediately concerned with the maintenance of blood volume as part of the internal environment of the body. But other hormones are intimately involved in this still largely mysterious story. The tubules of the kidney, and thus the excretion or conservation of water, are controlled by pitressin. Cortisol also plays a part. It raises the level of sodium and lowers that of potassium. Patients with Cushing's disease, whose secretion of cortisol is high, retain excessively both sodium and water in their bodies. Oestradiol, one of the natural hormones of the ovary, has a profound effect on water metabolism, retaining water in the body, and therefore in the blood, and patients have been precipitated into heart failure by the unwise use of synthetic oestrogens such as stilboestrol, the inefficient heart being incapable of forcing around the circulatory system an excessive volume of blood. The thyroid is also involved, water retention occurring in severe myxoedema.

Red cells

The solid constituents of the blood are affected also by the hormones. The kidney hormone erythropoietin is especially important. It controls the production of red cells by the bone marrow, being produced in a larger amount in anaemias of various kinds. In animal experiments an excessive number of red cells can be produced by its administration. In anaemia associated with disease of the kidney, changes in the bone marrow have been found, the production of red cells being depressed. Consistently high levels of erythropoietic hormone in the blood have been demonstrated in various forms of anaemia, suggesting an attempt by the kidneys to preserve the production of red cells at a proper level. Conversely in renal disease with anaemia, such high levels have not been found. Polycythaemia – an excessive number of red cells in the blood – may be due to several known causes, and is associated with a high level of erythropoietic hormone. Conversely in primary polycythaemia the level is low, presumably because its production by the kidney is suppressed.

Other hormones are concerned in erythropoiesis – the production of red blood cells. Long-standing testicular deficiency reduces the cellularity of the bone marrow, which can be restored to normal by treatment with androgens. Some cases of anaemia unresponsive to iron and liver respond to treatment with androgens, but in children treatment with cortisone must also be given to overcome the unduly rapid maturation of the epiphyses that androgens may occasionally cause. Anaemia is common in pituitary deficiency. This seems to have a complex origin. Such patients are lacking in androgens but also in thyroxine and cortisol, both of which affect erythropoiesis.

The thyroid is of special interest. In thyroid deficiency anaemia of several types may occur. The red cells may be large or small, packed with haemoglobin or lacking it. The bone marrow is often partially aplastic, and the production of red cells may be arrested in the early megaloblastic stage, when a macrocytic or large-celled anaemia occurs, or later, in the normoblastic stage, when cells of normal size are produced albeit in small numbers. These changes may be related to a surfeit of oxygen due to the small demands of other tissues. Sometimes, however, a condition of the blood is seen which is indistinguishable from pernicious anaemia. Recent research suggests that this type is due to the phenomenon rather unfortunately known as autoimmunity. The word really means 'immunity to self': it has come to mean, owing to the unfortunate ignorance of the classics common in scientific men, the exact opposite. It now implies a condition in which the body, far from being immune to its own constituents, comes to react against them. The first clear-cut example of this disorder to be clearly demonstrated was the thyroid disorder called Hashimoto's disease, in which, for a reason still only surmised, thyroglobulin and other normal constituents of the thyroid escape into the blood, in which they are not normally present, and there provoke a foreign-body reaction, a protective reaction against the strange invader somewhat similar to that provoked by foreign bodies in such allergic disorders as hay fever and asthma. Part of this reaction is the invasion of the thyroid by white blood cells, which strangle the normal cells and cause a deficiency of thyroxine. This in itself may cause anaemia but there is more to it than that. The tendency to autoimmune disease is in some individuals not confined to the thyroid. Such diseases often run in twos and threes. The patient may be affected by a similar disease in the mucous membrane of the stomach, with a consequent failure to produce hydrochloric acid and the 'intrinsic factor', the absence of which causes pernicious anaemia. The lack of hydrochloric acid causes a failure properly to absorb iron, a necessary part of haemoglobin. The lack of the intrinsic factor produces a severe anaemia that, before the discovery of the effects of liver extract and later of vitamin B12, ultimately caused death.

White cells

The white cells of the blood, the leucocytes, are also affected by hormones. Over a century ago, Thomas Addison noticed an excess of leucocytes in the blood of a patient with adrenal deficiency, and hypertrophy of the lymphoid tissues in another. In more recent years it has been found that corticotrophin and cortisone cause these tissues to shrink. They also cause a diminution in the number of some types of white cell. Though we are now sure that these changes are related to shocks and stresses of various kinds, we are still ignorant of the exact processes involved.

Much publicity has been given of late to the possible effects of contraceptive pills on the clotting mechanism of the blood. This is discussed fully in chapter 9.

20 Growth

The growth of a child is controlled in part by his genes. That there are tall families and short families, tall races and short races, is obvious. It is not known to what extent, if any, the influence of genes is exercised by way of the endocrine system. There is a race of mice in which dwarfism is genetic, the actual abnormality inherited being an absence of eosinophil cells, the source of growth hormone, in the anterior pituitary gland. Perhaps the same mechanism is at work in man. Pigmies, on the other hand, even though their level of growth hormone is apparently normal, fail to react to influences that would normally increase it.

But the growth hormone of the pituitary is not the only hormone involved. Almost every endocrine gland has its part to play. Moreover, diverse factors not obviously endocrine are associated with deficiency of growth, which is found in malnutrition, whether this is due to starvation or to disease of the bowel, vitamin deficiency such as rickets, congenital heart disease and disorders of the kidneys. Growth is often retarded in Hirschsprung's disease, a congenital disease of the lower bowel caused by an error in the development of the autonomic nervous system. Many illnesses in childhood may diminish the final height of the individual, for the sick child grows more slowly without any commensurate slowing of the rate of maturation of the bones. These mature at the expected time and growth ceases before the child has had a chance to catch up. Conversely it appears that stress in childhood may actually increase the rate of growth. Rats subjected to various stresses in the laboratory, such as rough handling, electric shocks or cold, grow faster than those more kindly treated. It is claimed that children of tribes that practise decorative scarring, circumcision or head-squeezing grow larger, but it is obviously difficult to eliminate other associated factors such as diet and genes. A better experiment compared the heights of vaccinated and unvaccinated children in a like environment: the vaccinated children grew larger, but why is still unknown.

Essentially growth is the result of a competition between anabolism, or building up of protein, and catabolism, or breaking down. Anabolism is assisted by growth hormone, insulin, thyroxine, and androgens. Catabolism is assisted by cortisol. In childhood, growth is determined by the first three of these. At puberty androgens, from the adrenals in both sexes and the testicles in the boy produce a spurt in growth. In girls, the increased activity of the ovaries at this time produces a rapid maturation of the bones and, after the initial spurt, a consequent slowing and ultimate cessation of growth. This is not so to the same extent in boys. Testosterone has a less potent effect on bony maturation. For this reason a boy often grows for five years or more after reaching puberty, whereas the girl rarely grows at all for more than a few months after her menstruation begins.

Growth of the long bones does not occur throughout their length. Each long bone has a shaft, the metastasis, with a knob at each end, the epiphysis, separated by a disc of cartilage or gristle. It is here that growth in length occurs. Gradually with time the cartilage ossifies and when ossification is complete no further increase in length is possible. The oestrogens, by hurrying this process, may be used to slow the growth of the girl who threatens to be excessively tall. The androgens, with their weaker activity in this respect, are less successful in halting the growth of the excessively tall boy. Nevertheless they are not entirely without effect, for in both sexes a very early puberty results in an individual with very short legs and arms proportionately to the total height.

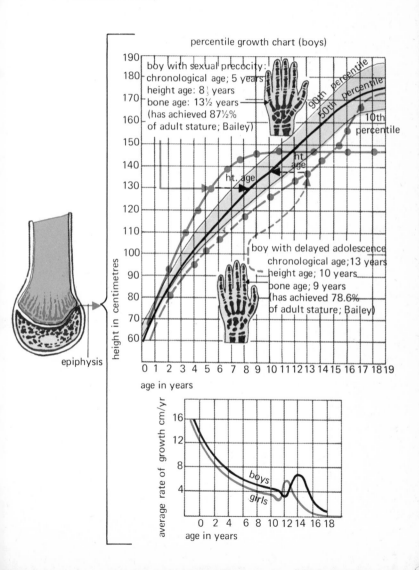

20·1 The effects of premature and delayed adolescence on growth. Premature puberty causes unduly early maturation of the epiphyses. There is therefore rapid growth and early cessation of growth. Delayed puberty retards growth and maturation of the epiphyses. There is therefore retarded growth until puberty occurs. If puberty is greatly retarded, growth may continue long enough to produce a boy of above average height. The effects of puberty in girls are similar to those in boys, but oestradiol has a stronger effect on the epiphyses and cessation of growth therefore occurs more rapidly after puberty.

percentile growth chart (boys)

boy with sexual precocity:
chronological age; 5 years
height age: 8½ years
bone age: 13½ years
(has achieved 87½%
of adult stature; Bailey)

90th percentile
50th percentile
10th percentile

ht. age

ht. age

boy with delayed adolescence
chronological age; 13 years
height age; 10 years
bone age; 9 years
(has achieved 78.6%
of adult stature; Bailey)

height in centimetres

age in years

epiphysis

average rate of growth cm/yr

boys

girls

age in years

20·2 The normal growth pattern of girls. The dashed curves cover the period of adolescence.

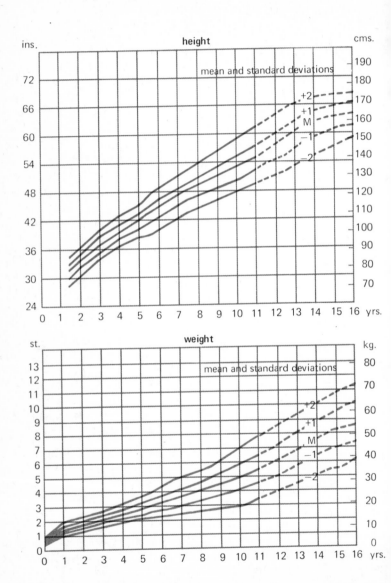

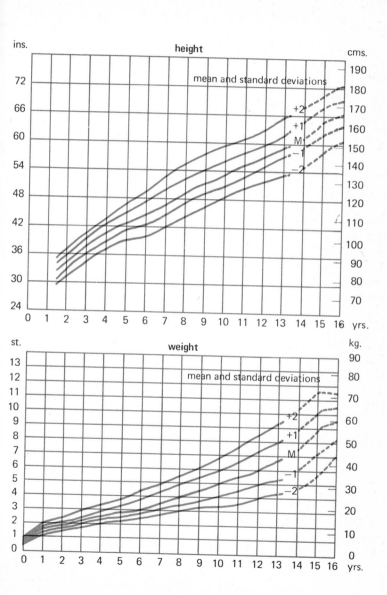

ins.   height   cms.

weight

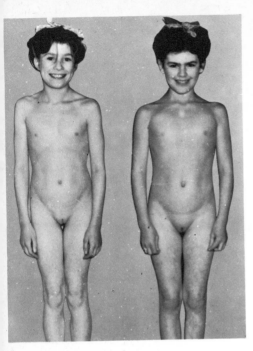

20·4 Left Hypopituitarism. These two girls of sixteen are small for lack of growth hormone and have failed in sexual development for lack of gonadotrophin.

20·5 Right The Irish Giant, who presumably had an excessive production of growth hormone in childhood. The overproduction burned itself out before the epiphyses matured, for otherwise he would have become acromegalic as well as gigantic.

As we saw in chapter 3, growth hormone is secreted by the eosinophil cells of the anterior pituitary. When there is a tumour of these cells in childhood, the child becomes a giant. When the disease occurs in adult years, the epiphyses have already united with the metaphyses of the long bones and an extension in length is impossible. Therefore the growth hormone causes excessive growth in any way it can, in breadth of bones instead of length and in excessive growth of soft tissue. This is the disease called acromegaly. Conversely when the activity of the acidophil cells of the pituitary is subnormal, usually because of a tumour pressing upon them, the child remains unduly small and in adult years is a dwarf. When pituitary deficiency exists from birth, the failure to grow is obvious very early in life. In addition, the face remains childish, there is retarded development of the skele-

20·6 Left Sir Geoffrey Hudson, by Mytens. Sir Geoffrey was 18 ins high at the age of nine and 45 ins at thirty. He had a distinguished diplomatic career in the reign of Charles I, killed an adversary in a duel, was captured and enslaved by Moorish pirates, escaped, and died at the age of sixty-three in receipt of a royal pension. It is reported that he grew during the privations of his captivity, which may have been due to a temporary reactivation of the growth hormone releasing factor.

20·7 Right A pituitary dwarf, aged ten, and his twin sister.

ton and ultimately in most cases secondary deficiency of other endocrine glands becomes obvious. Rarely, however, an isolated deficiency of growth hormone occurs, the pituitary continuing to exercise its control over the other glands.

Apart from organic disease of the pituitary we have recently learned a lot about the control of the output of growth hormone. It is increased by a low blood sugar, and therefore by an excess of insulin and decreased by an excess of cortisol. Children with asthma treated by cortisone or similar hormones fail to grow normally. Emotional and psychological factors may depress the output of growth hormone and such children begin to grow naturally when their environment is improved. It would seem that emotional trauma may act by way of the hypothalamus.

Growth hormone differs from other pituitary hormones in having no target gland. Whereas thyrotrophin acts mainly

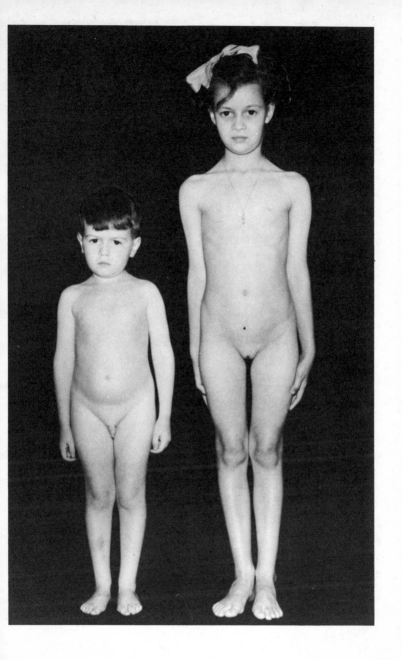

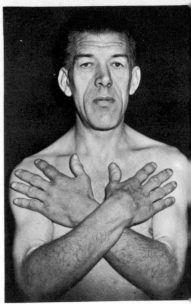

on the thyroid, corticotrophin on the adrenal cortex and gonadotrophin on the ovaries and testicles, growth hormone acts on every tissue of the body. It influences the metabolism of protein, carbohydrate and fats. Its full activity needs the partnership of insulin, thyroxine and testosterone. It causes the retention of substances needed for growth, such as nitrogen, phosphorus, potassium and calcium.

Children whose dwarfism is proved to be due to a deficiency of growth hormone respond well to treatment. Results are less certain when the cause of the failure to grow are less certain, and accurate diagnosis, often involving elaborate biochemical tests, is therefore important. Even in some cases in which the deficiency is not proven, improvement occasionally occurs. Unfortunately growth hormone has not been synthesised and all supplies have to be obtained from human pituitaries removed at necropsy: it is therefore in very short supply. Animal growth hormone does not work in humans.

20·8 Acromegaly, showing the characteristic changes in the facial appearance due to the development of a pituitary tumour.

217

However, pending the arrival of a synthetic growth hormone, much may be done by the use of the so-called anabolic hormones. Of these we have methyl testosterone, a synthetic near relation of the natural testosterone, and other synthetic substances with an equal effect on growth but a smaller masculinising effect. It is usual to use the first in boys who in addition to small size have poor sexual development, and the second group in boys whose sexual development is normal. Although the masculinising effect is very slight it is not completely absent and even the so-called 'non-virilising hormones' must be used in girls with great caution. In both sexes care must be taken to ensure that the drug used does not produce unduly rapid bony maturation and consequent cessation of growth. This complication of treatment is, however, rare, and the effect on growth is at least as good as that of human growth hormone. It has been suggested that the anabolic drugs produce their effect by increasing the output of growth hormone by the pituitary, but the biochemical changes are not completely identical.

The anabolic steroids have recently come into prominence because of their use by athletes, who hope thereby to increase their muscular prowess. It is said that their muscles become larger, though this has not been proved by experiment. Moreover there is no evidence that larger muscles are necessarily more efficient.

The effect of the thyroid on growth is a complex one. In the first place thyroid deficiency causes the disappearance of growth hormone in rats and in humans interferes with the response of growth hormone to insulin. Yet cretins produce normal amounts of growth hormone and their short stature must be ascribed to other causes. A direct effect of thyroxine seems probable. In the hypothyroid child all development, eruption of teeth, growth of the skull and long bones, bony development, and even the intelligence, is retarded. Conversely the growth and general development of the hyperthyroid child are accelerated.

Diabetic children tend to grow unduly slowly, and excessively slowly in one rare type of the disease known as pseudophlorhizin diabetes. The situation is complicated by the fact that an excess of growth hormone can itself cause diabetes in adults. By inhibiting the oxidation of glucose it causes growth in the young, diabetes in the old. Women who are fated to develop diabetes later tend to have excessively large babies. The reason for this is unknown. It has been suggested, but never proved, that they carry an excess of growth hormone that affects the foetus before it has had time to affect the mother.

That there was a relationship between hormones and cancer had been realised, albeit dimly, from the time of John Hunter (1728–93) who noticed that some forms of enlargement of the prostate gland were benefited by castration. We now realise that this benefit was achieved only in malignant enlargement. A gap of a century intervened before Beatson, in 1896, claimed that removal of the ovaries slowed the progress of cancer of the breast. Further progress had to await more recent advances in the science of endocrinology.

During recent years an enormous variety of facts have been established but we are still far from a general theory about the relationship of the endocrines to malignant growths. We have learned that many tumours are, temporarily at any rate, under endocrine control. Huggins showed in 1941 that cancer of the prostate may be temporarily suppressed by treatment with oestrogens. Certain kinds of thyroid cancer may be relieved, some would say permanently, by thyroxine. Cancer of the breast in mice of an especially susceptible strain is induced by oestrogens, but there is no proof that this is true of women. The removal of the pituitary and adrenals is widely used in the treatment of cancer of the breast and temporary improvement, alas only temporary, is undoubtedly seen. It may be doubted whether the results justify the means: a prolongation of the patient's illness and the continuing anxiety of her relations is a high price to pay for a few months of life. It seems that a tumour is for a time embarrassed by a change in its hormonal environment but ultimately adjusts itself to this and continues its onward course, achieving an autonomy so complete that it is free from any kind of endocrine control. This may sound pessimistic but the fact that tumours can be embarrassed, albeit temporarily, by changes in their endocrine environment, holds out some hope that a time may come when a more effective environmental change may be possible and a major scourge eliminated.

We do not yet know whether any hormone initiates cancer. It may well be that it does not, and indeed it seems improbable that it should. If no other cause is operating we would expect that everyone under the influence of that hormone would develop cancer. True, in animal experiments, hormones have been shown to 'initiate' cancers, but only when administered in doses to which the human being is unlikely to be submitted. It seems possible that many cancers are really initiated by some other cause but encouraged or discouraged by their hormonal environment. It is known that a very high proportion of the prostates of elderly men contain small lumps of malignant tissue, discovered by accident at post mortem examination. That they have caused no trouble to their hosts may perhaps be due to the fact that testosterone, known to exacerbate prostatic cancer, is secreted in diminishing amounts by the elderly testicle.

In thinking of the possibility that hormones actually initiate cancer we must consider the fact that they have a deleterious effect only in those organs in which they are necessary for normal growth and development, for instance oestrogens in the breast, androgens in the prostate. It is an interesting fact that even when enormous doses of oestrogens are given to mice with a genetic tendency to develop cancer, the stimulus must be continuous. If the same total dose is given in alternate periods of five days, those given interrupted treatment are no more likely to develop cancer of the breast than the untreated animals. Perhaps it is a happy thing that oestrogens in women are cyclically secreted, reaching their highest (but not very high) level at fortnightly intervals. In women, hormone dependence remains mysterious, and the mystery is increased by the probability that we are wrong to think too much about oestrogens. The removal of the pituitary or adrenal glands may produce temporary alleviation even when no oestrogen is detectable before operation and even when the operation fails to eliminate oestrogen altogether. The other glands are probably involved. Workers at the Imperial Cancer Research Fund laboratories have shown that patients differ in their excretion of certain steroids. When these are present in a certain proportion, hypophysectomy or adrenalectomy are likely to be helpful, for the cancer is 'hormone dependent'. When they are present in a different proportion, operation is useless – the growth is 'hormone-independent'.

The reason behind the removal of the pituitary gland is that the operation removes the stimulus the pituitary provides to other glands. To remove it implies that all other endocrine glands, with the exception of the parathyroids, go to rest, but not necessarily into a deep sleep. If we assume that cancer of the breast is initiated or even encouraged by other hormones, pituitary or pituitary-dependent, the operation makes sense. The pituitary hormone most likely to be concerned is prolactin but the interpretation of its hormonal control of the breast is complicated by the fact that it is itself 'luteotropic' – it increases the secretion of progesterone. Probably all three hormones oestradiol, progesterone and prolactin are necessary for the normal development of the breast and perhaps for the abnormal development, the incidence or anyway the encouragement of cancer. Ablation of the pituitary deprives the body of growth hormone, the significance of which in the breast is still uncertain. Even the posterior lobe may be important, because one of its hormones, oxytocin, encourages the release of prolactin. The thyroid may also be involved, for it is claimed that rats with hypothyroidism are more sensitive to the actions of oestradiol and progesterone. The actions of any one hormone cannot be considered in isolation. Removal of the pituitary is a blunderbuss operation that reduces the production of pituitary, gonadal and adrenal hormones, but it does not necessarily eliminate altogether the last two sets. In any case the rather drastic operations of complete removal of the pituitary or the adrenals have no effect on the progress of cancers other than those of the breast and prostate. Even in these the results are temporary.

It seems, therefore, that many hormones may in some mysterious way be able to modify the growth of tumours. The question then arises of how they do this. Apart from the rather subtle changes in adrenocortical function described by the Imperial Cancer Research Fund workers, no abnormality of the endocrine status has been detected in patients with cancer. It seems possible that the liver plays some part in the mystery. It is known to inactivate oestrogens. Damage to the liver by a deficiency of protein or of vitamin B in the diet may be important. There is a high incidence of mammary cancer, a very rare male disease in most countries, in Bantu man, whose diet is deficient in both these substances. It has been claimed that in Canada there is an association between vitamin B deficiency and cancer of the neck of the womb.

Research on cancer is being conducted intensively on many fronts. Studies in biology, genetics and immunology are yielding new clues every year. These studies are not, and cannot be, conducted in isolation and it is probable that at least one connecting link between them is endocrinology, a study that has already produced results of some, albeit slight, practical use.

22 Allergy and infection

The first indication of the importance of a hormone in infection was the disastrous effect at first of treating with cortisone patients already infected with tuberculosis, yet further study has shown that this effect may be on the contrary beneficial and steroid hormones are now actually used in the treatment of this disease.

Soon after the introduction of cortisone in 1946, a patient with Addison's disease and pulmonary tuberculosis was admitted to the Royal Northern Hospital. In the past a fairly successful treatment was by means of the steroid DOCA (desoxycorticosterone acetate), which restored the disturbed electrolyte balance of the body, raising to normal the level of sodium in the blood. However it had no effect upon the low level of glucose. The patient in question, despite the correction of his sodium level, began to have episodes of coma due to lack of glucose. This could, of course, be corrected by infusions of glucose, but repeated infusions were hardly compatible with a normal life at home. It was known that cortisone could raise the blood sugar, but it was also known that it could cause a severe attack of tuberculosis. In this dilemma it was decided to treat the tuberculosis with streptomycin and to add cortisone only when the body was 'flooded' with the antibiotic, the principle being 'to use cortisone to set fire to the hay rick and to shoot the tubercle bacilli with streptomycin when they ran out'. This rather drastic experiment was successful. The patient was cured of tuberculosis and his Addison's disease was controlled from both points of view of the sodium and glucose levels.

The main effect of the adrenal steroids in infectious disease is the suppression of the inflammatory responses of the body, including the phagocytic action of the white blood cells, the repair processes (by the formation of fibrous tissue and the formation of granulation tissue) and the production of anti-bodies. In consequence they have a superficially beneficent effect, for many of the symptoms of an illness are produced by the reaction to it rather than by the illness itself. Thus fever is abolished, whereas the underlying disease continues with increased vigour. In tuberculosis any tendency for the disease to become localised comes to an end and the bacilli multiply more rapidly. In tuberculous meningitis, an invariably fatal disease in the era before antibiotics, death after their introduction was due to the fibrous tissue, formed during healing, blocking the circulation of cerebrospinal fluid. Cortisone, given in addition to antibiotic therapy, prevents this excessive formation of fibrous tissue and results in cure in many cases.

In pulmonary tuberculosis the combined treatment with antibiotics and steroids results in an improved sense of well-being, increase in weight, and quicker changes in x-ray appearances. These benefits are obtained at a price and a careful watch is necessary lest the side effects of cortisone should occur, such as 'mooning' of the face, diabetes, and ulcers of the stomach or duodenum.

There exists a large group of obscure diseases to which the name 'collagen disease' has been applied. The best known of these is rheumatoid arthritis. The real basis of the trouble in this group has still to be found, but there is no doubt that the so-called immune reactions of the body are in some way involved. Some believe that the reactions to stress described in chapter 4 have in some way gone wrong. In the case of rheumatoid arthritis some point is given to the hypothesis by the curious variety of apparent 'causes' such as fatigue, injuries, the endocrine stresses of puberty, pregnancy and the menopause, drug sensitivity, allergy and even psychological disturbances. That the adrenal cortex might in some way be involved was suggested in the nineteen thirties and various adrenal extracts were used unsuccessfully.

Cortisone has proved a life-saving drug in several diseases, especially in disseminated lupus, and a useful one in nephritis, psoriasis, pemphigus, and the various allergic disorders. The symptoms of a disease are due in part to the direct action of the attacker and in part to the reaction of the attacked, which may be inappropriately violent. Cortisone abolishes these violent reactions, such as those which occur in allergic diseases, which may often be greatly relieved by the administration of cortisone-like drugs, even by means of a cream for the skin or snuff for the nose.

The fact that cortisone, involved undoubtedly in the response of the body to stress, is useful to a limited extent in certain diseases, does not of course prove that in these diseases the response to stress has failed. Today a more fashionable attempt to explain such diseases is based on the concept of autoimmunity. Addison's disease, when it is not due to tuberculosis, falls into this category. 'Auto-antibodies' to organs can now be detected in the blood of such patients and are in effect revolutionary troops bent on attacking essential organs of the body. Often several separate regiments with different objectives are detectable, bent on attacking the thyroid, for example, and causing Hashimoto's disease; the glands of the stomach, causing pernicious anaemia; the thymus, causing myasthenia gravis; the parathyroid glands, causing calcium deficiency; perhaps the islets of Langerhans, causing diabetes mellitus. Rheumatoid arthritis may belong to this group of diseases.

Allergy is an overworked word. It is used here to imply the production of a specific disease, such as asthma, hay fever, eczema and others known and perhaps unknown, by contact with a substance, usually a protein, which is harmless to most people. Several hormones are capable of modifying allergy: thyroxine and cortisone have opposite effects, the former increasing and the latter inhibiting allergic manifestations. The use of cortisone in allergic diseases is the more valuable because in many it may be used locally and for short periods only, thus diminishing the fear of dangerous side effects.

It has been suggested by Zondek, the great Israeli endocrinologist, that the body may be adversely affected by its own hormones. He claimed that sensitivity to oestrogens may cause asthma, premenstrual tension, and pruritus vulvae; to progesterone, migraine; and to testosterone, the distressing skin condition rosacea. These claims have not been altogether substantiated but equally they have never been disproved. Thought at first to be an improbable hypothesis, some credence has been added to his view by the fact, since established beyond cavil, that the body may indeed become sensitive to its own thyroglobulin.

The effects of hormones on inflammation are at present the subject of intense research that is likely to prove of even greater use in the treatment of diseases bearing in the past no obvious relationship to the endocrine system.

The activity of yet another adrenal hormone, adrenaline itself, has been for many years of the greatest practical use in allergic conditions. It produces a prompt response in every attack of hay fever by overcoming the congestion of the nose and eyes and is commonly of use in asthma not only by decongestion but by relief of bronchospasm. In the very acute and dangerous form of allergy called anaphylaxis, such as that which occurs in previously sensitised individuals when horse serum is given to prevent tetanus, adrenaline may be life-saving.

Before we discuss where hormones come into the enormous and important field of rheumatism, we must decide what we mean by this very vague word. Everybody has his own view of what it means. To the doctor it means almost nothing, but the highest common factor in its interpretation is probably a chronic pain in one of the supporting structures of the body, bones, joints, ligaments or muscles, that is not explained by some acute disease. For the doctor it has come to mean mainly osteoarthritis, rheumatoid arthritis and a large number of less common and less well-defined entities. The 'muscular rheumatism' of ordinary conversation usually means a pain, apparently situated in a muscle, that is usually referred from a joint, most commonly spinal, affected by osteoarthritis, a degenerative disease due to acute injury or to the wear and tear of time. We know of no hormonal relationship. The 'fibrositis' of which our patients tell us, often informed by their masseuse, belongs to this category; there is no evidence of any of that inflammation of fibrous tissue that the name implies.

Rheumatoid arthritis is very different. It is a general disease of the body, usually chiefly manifest in joints, especially, at the beginning, those of the hands. It has many biochemical and haematological characteristics. Unlike osteoarthritis, it is common in the young. It has for long been suspected of being related to the adrenal glands, largely because of the manner in which it tends to vary in relation to the stress of life. Thus it may begin at puberty or the menopause, or at times of great mental strain or during severe infections. It may remit completely during pregnancy, or during an attack of jaundice. Many crude adrenal extracts were tested by many investigators unsuccessfully, but in 1946 Mario and Guido Bassi of Bologna produced an extract of

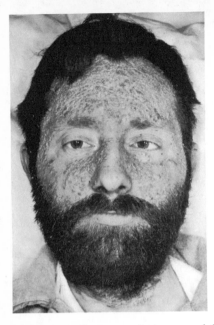

23·1 Rheumatoid arthritis. The patient, whose face shows the characteristic rash sometimes seen in severe rheumatoid arthritis, was the first to be treated with corticotrophin. He made a complete recovery, but needed increasing doses of corticotrophin, and later of cortisone, to remain free from pain. He ultimately died from the side effects of cortisone treatment.

the adrenal cortex that proved beneficial. In the same year Greene in London used an early sample of corticotrophin in a moribund patient with complete success. Two years later Hench and his colleagues at the Mayo Clinic were the first to use cortisone, with such success that enthusiasm for this treatment swept the world. The workers at Rochester deservedly received a Nobel Prize, but, especially in America where the drug was sold freely, many patients died from the still unrealised side effects.

But rheumatoid arthritis is not a sign of adrenal deficiency. It is not especially common in Addison's disease. The success of cortisone is pharmacological and not physiological. We still do not know the cause of rheumatoid arthritis but it seems probable that it results from a disturbance of the immune mechanisms of the body, related to allergy and especially to the autoimmune group of diseases.

The wonder drug has not retained its early reputation in the treatment of rheumatoid arthritis. In some patients, such as Greene's first case, increasing doses were necessary to maintain mobility until at last the side effects won. Nevertheless, it is not, as some pundits would have us believe, just a dangerous and expensive alternative to aspirin. The young patient, mildly afflicted, may sometimes be kept well by doses too small to produce side effects, and it must always be remembered that rheumatoid arthritis is a disease that may burn itself out. If the patient's joints can be kept mobile and undeformed during the initial years, they may ultimately remain normal without treatment. The hopelessly deformed and helpless old woman so commonly seen is usually suffering not from active disease but from the scars remaining from her past suffering.

Therefore the hope of the physician is to conduct the rheumatoid patient through the active phase of the disease, by corticosteroid or other medical treatment, by splinting, exercises and electrotherapy, to the time when no active treatment is needed and she may return to normal life with joints only mildly deformed and their function only mildly impaired.

24 Adiposity

Adiposity, let there be no doubt about it, is important not only aesthetically. It is not just a question of 'Nobody loves a fat girl, but gee how a fat girl can love', and in doing so experience terrible frustration. Nor does its importance rest in the undoubted fact that many women regard the fat man with amused contempt. Adiposity is a lethal disease, as every life assurance association knows. The fat man is especially liable to arteriosclerosis, hypertension, strokes, coronary disease and diabetes. Curiously enough, this is less true of the fat woman. She may be protected by her circulating oestrogens or there may be genetic influences at work. Nevertheless she also tends to live less long. She also is restricted in her physical capacity, tires easily because of the weight of useless blubber she must bear, often has a miserable feeling of inferiority, has flat feet and osteoarthritis, and has an unpleasant tendency to excessive sweating (about which her best friends do not tell her). Both sexes have an increased tendency to bronchitis.

The importance of adiposity is well shown in table 1 opposite. When the age of the 'life' is considered, the influence of adiposity becomes still more obvious, as shown in tables 2 and 3. In other words, a mere stone of extra weight in middle age lessens a man's expectation of life by about ten per cent, and fifty pounds overweight at age 45 imposes as much extra mortality as valvular heart disease.

There has been a revolution in thought about adiposity in recent years. Until perhaps fifteen years ago, the problem was considered to be one of simple arithmetic; 'If a person is fat, it is invariably because he eats too much. If he is thin it is because he eats too little.' A famous authority whose name it would now be unkind to mention called forth loud applause from an audience at the Royal Society of Medicine

Table 1 Influence of weight on mortality

Weight	Deaths per 100,000
Standard	844
Underweight	848
Overweight	1,111
Overweight 5-14%	1,027
Overweight 15-24%	1,215
Overweight 25% and over	1,472

Table 2 Influence of weight on mortality

Weight	Age	
	Under 45	Over 45
Standard	463	1,308
Underweight	498	1,274
Overweight	527	1,824

Table 3 Influence of overweight on mortality in persons aged 45 to 50

Pounds Overweight	Increase in Death Rate over Average
10	8
20	18
30	28
40	45
50	56
60	67
70	81
90	116

24·1 The effects on the blood sugar of protein, fat, and carbohydrate food. The red line shows how protein produces a slow increase in blood sugar, which persists for three or four hours. ('Meat stays by you'.) Carbohydrate produces a rapid rise in blood sugar followed in an hour or so by a reactive drop due to the increase in insulin secretion. Hunger and weakness cause a desire for more carbohydrate. The effect of fat is intermediate.

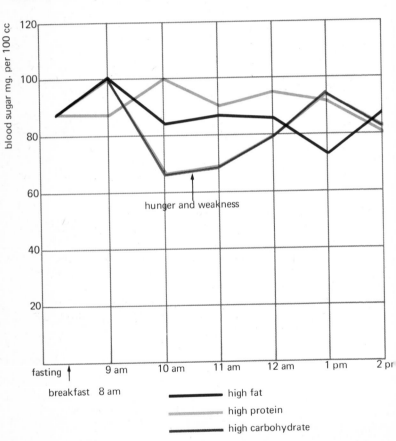

with the remark: 'When a patient says to me "Doctor, I have the appetite of a bird," I reply "Yes, madam, of a vulture".' The members of his audience were delighted to sail into the waters of security piloted by so eminent a physician. But, of course, he was talking nonsense. The suppression of inconvenient evidence is an old trick in the medical profession. The subterfuge may be due to love of a beautiful but unsound hypothesis but often enough it is due to a subconscious desire to simplify a confusing subject. There are even those who say, if not openly at least in their hearts: 'If I do not understand it, it isn't true.'

Of course, fat must come from food. Even the most vegetable-like of patients fail to abstract it from the circumambient air as leguminoseae abstract nitrogen. But since medical research workers have come at last to admit that there is a mystery about obesity, it has become respectable to admit that some people put on weight more easily than others and lose it when dieted with greater difficulty. This fact has always been known to observant clinicians; it has now been placed on a proper scientific basis, a phrase which means that it has been observed by people who are not clinicians and are therefore in their own view more trustworthy observers. In the last few years a genuine effort has been made to explain along metabolic lines the mysterious difference between fat and thin people who eat about the same amount.

Fat is laid down in adipose tissue, which was until recently regarded as a static store, but is now known to be far from static. It has a blood supply greater than that of muscle and is innervated by sympathetic nerve fibres. Its distribution is a very individual matter presumably determined before birth, though there may be exceptions to this rule. Thus of people of the same weight some have most of their fat above the waist (upper segment obesity) and some below (lower segment obesity). Some have fat legs and some thin ones. One patient has been recorded who was fat down one side of her body and thin on the other. Some African races are conspicuous for the enormous size of their bottoms. Many even more bizarre distributions of fat are occasionally observed and grouped together under the name of lipodystrophy.

The amount of food consumed and thus made available for ultimate conversion into fat is controlled by the appetite. In most people there is a remarkable balance between energy taken in as food and expended in activity, so that their weights remain fairly constant. This balance is controlled by the hypothalamus. There is a 'feeding centre' in the ventro-lateral region and a 'satiety centre' in the ventromedial region. A high rate of glucose utilisation activates the satiety centre which generates nervous impulses that inhibit the feeding centre. In addition to this mechanism various hormones influence the balance, including the adrenal steroids, adrenaline, growth hormone, oestrogen, thyroxine, glucagon and especially insulin.

It has often been stressed by research workers in this field that stimulation of the appetite centre in the hypothalamus causes obesity in experimental animals by producing 'polyphagia', an excessive intake of food. Clinicians have sometimes doubted this simple statement. Patients, some of whom have suffered known damage to their brains by accident or infection, sometimes grow fat without any obvious increase in appetite and may be remarkably resistant to slimming diets. In one inbred strain of mice, animals put on twenty-five per cent more weight than normal controls even when given the same amount of food. They have also very high levels of

blood sugar and of insulin, but are relatively insensitive to their own and to administered insulin. Another interesting thing about these mice is that in youth their adipose tissue only responds to insulin by absorbing glucose and not their muscles, whereas in normal mice both tissues respond. When the obese mice are a year old, a change occurs, their adipose tissue fails to respond, and their weight levels out. It may be that a similar condition is present in some humans.

The hypothalamic mechanism is of two kinds, a short-term day-by-day one that adapts the appetite to the energy output, and a long-term one that corrects any errors of the short-term one. The short-term mechanism works with

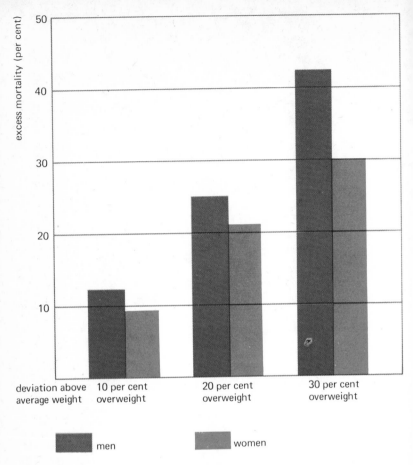

excess mortality (per cent)

deviation above average weight | 10 per cent overweight | 20 per cent overweight | 30 per cent overweight

men   women

considerable precision as a general rule but becomes deranged in sedentary states and during excessive exercise, in which the individual is liable to lay down excessive fat or to lose his stores. For long it was considered that the controlling influence over hypothalamic mechanisms was the gastric contraction that occurs in hunger, but this was shown to be incorrect. Filling the stomach with an inert material abolishes the gastric hunger contractions but makes little or no difference to the food intake, a fact that makes nonsense of the

24·3 The effect of obesity on mortality. Obesity is a killing disease, especially in men.

237

treatment of obesity with methyl cellulose so common today. Moreover, cutting the nerves to the stomach (vagotomy) abolishes gastric contractions without diminishing hunger.

The hypothalamic mechanism of fat control, like many other hypothalamic functions, may be disturbed by psychological means. Helen Bruch, the eminent American psychologist, once wrote: 'show me a fat child and I will show you a disturbed home' or words to that effect. Often the fat child has been coddled unduly: sweets have been used as rewards and deprivation of sweets as punishment. Unhappiness from any cause may lead to the child finding gratification and comfort in food, and not only the child. Just as many an adult man will say: 'I'm fed up, I'm going to have a drink,' so his wife will raid the larder, choosing always food needing little or no preparation such as cake or bread and jam.

The endocrine aspects of obesity, for long in the doldrums, are now being subjected to careful studies but these are still in an early stage. Much dead wood has been discarded. It was, for instance, fashionable to speak of 'pituitary obesity' or obesity due to pituitary deficiency. This erroneous idea arose through the study of Frölich's syndrome, a condition in which a tumour of the anterior pituitary progressively destroys its function on the one hand and on the other affects the hypothalamus above. It is now realised that the obesity that is a prominent feature of the syndrome is due not to pituitary destruction but to interference with hypothalamic function. Indeed in Simmonds' disease and Sheehan's syndrome, in which the pituitary is destroyed by thrombosis of its blood vessels, obesity does not necessarily or commonly occur. Hyperpituitarism likewise cannot be linked with obesity. Acromegalics in general are not inclined to be fat, and obese patients tend to have less growth hormone in their

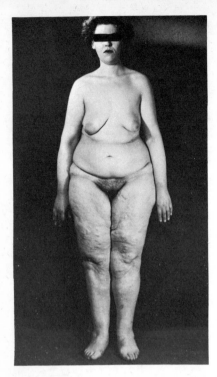

24·4 Lipodystrophy. Most of the adipose tissue lies in the part of the body below the waist. In consequence, the torso is normal.

blood than thin ones, even when fasting. Obese patients have a normal response to injected growth hormone. Lately a fashion has grown up of injecting obese patients with chorionic gonadotrophin, combining this with a 500 calorie diet. There is no sound logic behind this treatment and no properly controlled trials have been made. It is probable that the loss of weight occurs solely because of the diet, adhered to with greater zeal because of the necessity of frequent visits to the doctor prescribing it.

More attention has been given to the pituitary by Kekwick and his colleagues at the Middlesex Hospital. They found that when they gave patients a diet that provided 1,000 calories, the loss of weight depended on the proportion of fat to carbohydrate. When the diet contained ninety per cent of fat or of protein, weight was lost faster than when it contained ninety per cent of carbohydrate. With the high fat and high protein diets, but not with the high carbohydrate diet, they detected in the urine a substance that mobilised fatty acids from adipose tissue *in vitro*. The substance caused loss of fat in mice and inhibited the ability of adipose tissue to form fat from carbohydrate. The suggestion was made that this substance is of pituitary origin but it is not, apparently, one of the known pituitary hormones. Clinicians have long believed that carbohydrate should be restricted in obese patients and the Middlesex work gives scientific support to their views. Other workers have found that whereas total fasting causes twice as great a loss of lean tissue compared with fat, a high fat diet of 1,000 calories causes a loss of only three per cent of lean tissue. In one experiment total starvation for ten days caused a mean loss of 9·6 kilograms, of which 6·2 kilograms were lean tissue and 3·4 kilograms fat. On the contrary a 1,000 calorie high fat diet caused a somewhat smaller loss of 6·6 kilograms of which all was fat save an insignificant 0·2 kilograms of lean tissue. In another experiment a 1,000 calorie diet high in protein with a normal fat content and a very low carbohydrate one produced results as good as total starvation.

The thyroid gland has also had its share of blame. There is some apparently good logical basis for the treatment of obese patients with thyroxine, but unless the gland is deficient the logic is only *apparently* good. In the first place, obese patients are not necessarily hypothyroid, though some undoubtedly are. If their thyroid function is normal, the administration of thyroxine in physiological doses sets in motion the thyroid-pituitary servo-mechanism and the *status quo* is rapidly restored. When excessive doses are given the patient is, indeed, likely to lose weight, as the thyrotoxic patient usually does, but the loss is of muscle as well as of fat, and this is clearly not desirable. The patient is subjected, too, to all the hazards of the thyrotoxic state, including damage to the heart. Even when the treatment is discontinued, the thyrotoxicosis may persist. On the other hand, if the patient is deficient in thyroid secretion, treatment with thyroxine is desirable. The metabolism is stimulated, so that a given amount of exercise balances a larger amount of food and the diuretic effect of thyroxine produces a diminution in the excessive tissue fluid characteristic of myxoedema. It must however be remembered that thyroxine is a stimulant to the appetite, a fact that explains the increase in weight occasionally seen in Graves' disease. A satisfactory result in the treatment with thyroxine of obesity in hypothyroid patients can only be expected if a strict diet is concurrently followed.

The adrenal cortex is certainly concerned in the problem of obesity. People with Cushing's syndrome, in which an excessive amount of cortisol is secreted by the adrenals, are usually fat. The explanation of this is thought to lie in the capacity of cortisol to produce gluconeogenesis, the conversion of protein into glucose, which is then deposited as fat in the adipose tissue. More doubt exists about the explanation of the curious fact that obese patients who are not suffering from Cushing's syndrome often have an abnormal level of adrenal hormones in their urine, and may even have the purple stretch marks on the skin so typical of the disease. Some people think that obesity comes first and causes stress and hence adrenal overactivity; others wonder whether this explanation is too facile. Could not the adrenal overactivity come first?

The role of the sex glands in adiposity is not well understood. It is, of course, common knowledge that castration of various farm animals leads to increased fat, and the popular view of the eunuch pictures him as obese, though he often is not. Women often tend to put on weight after the change of life, but by no means constantly. Perhaps people with no gonads are for some reason less active than others. Perhaps, too, some people become more interested in food when their libido diminishes: 'lip to lip while we're young, then the lip to the glass,' as John Gay wrote.

The pancreas is the most important of all the glands in adiposity. We have already seen that the appetite centres in the hypothalamus respond to the level of glucose in the blood. An excessive production of insulin by the pancreas, by lowering this, increases the desire for food. Many obese people tend for one reason or another to have a rather low blood sugar and in attempting to correct this become unduly fat. They often make the mistake of eating a lot of sugar. This raises the blood sugar rapidly, producing an immediate sense of relief, but the sudden rise in blood sugar causes a sudden secretion of insulin, the blood sugar falls rapidly and the desire to eat returns. If they eat protein in the form of animal food and completely abjure sugar, there is a slower, less dramatic but more lasting rise in the sugar level in the blood.

The study of insulin levels has shown that this increases after a glucose feed more in the obese than in the slim, especially if they are not diabetic. Third in order of this increment come the normal people who are neither obese nor diabetic. Last come the thin diabetics who are incapable of producing more than a feeble rise. The relationship of obesity to diabetes should act as a warning against gluttony. Despite their ability to secrete insulin, fifty per cent of obese people are diabetic; conversely seventy-five per cent of people who become diabetic in middle age are obese. It may seem surprising that individuals so good at secreting insulin should be diabetic. The answer to the conundrum lies in the fact that their tissues do not respond to insulin in a normal way, but why we do not know. Perhaps they harbour in their cells an antidote to insulin. Perhaps further studies of genetically obese mice may provide an answer.

The effects of lethargy and of exercise in the production and relief of obesity have been much debated. On the one hand it has been stated on high authority that the effects of playing tennis for half an hour are offset in terms of calories by an extra sandwich or a dry martini. On the other hand it may be argued that the experiment is too acute. Of more interest is the total twenty-four hour activity. We have already seen that the hypothalamic balance may be upset in the sedentary and exhaustion ranges. It is not always realised how little exercise many people take. Young military cadets, who take what would be regarded as a lot of physical exercise, spend an average of $17\frac{3}{4}$ hours a day lying down, sitting, or standing still. Coal miners even, possibly the hardest physical workers in the community, spend $18\frac{3}{4}$ hours in a similar way and, at the other end of the scale, colliery clerks 20 hours. The obese have a decided tendency to move about little and slowly. Obese children especially have an extremely low level of activity. Careful statistical investigation has shown that obese children eat less than slim ones, but exercise strikingly less, and there is evidence that inactivity precedes excessive weight gain. The cause of the initial inactivity may be illness, psychological or organic. Illness in children enters the picture also through parental concern – 'you must eat well darling and get strong again.' The habit of overeating during convalescence may be perpetuated, partly by habit and partly by the initiation of sedentary habits. In this connection it seems rarely to be realised how unsound is the measurement of metabolism by the standard BMR test, usually carried out in the early morning after a night of sound sleep. It is the total energy expended throughout the twenty-four hours that really counts. Some people have extremely low metabolism during sleep and appear in fact almost to hibernate. Such people must be more than normally active by day to compensate for this, but they rarely are. It is quite likely that, as we have seen, the relationship between weight and food intake is somewhat vague but the relationship between weight and activity clearer.

So far we have talked in what may appear to the reader a rather old-fashioned way, in terms of the calorie value of food eaten and of energy expended. But man does not eat calories. He eats proteins, fats, carbohydrates, minerals and vitamins. Studies of the different effects of the first three on body weight have been mentioned. The question of when and how often food is eaten must be considered also. It is said, and disputed, that with the same intake of calories larger infrequent meals ('meal eating') cause less loss of weight than smaller frequent ones ('nibbling'), and that both in laboratory animals and human patients 'meal eating' encourages storage of fat whereas 'nibbling' discourages it. Here the type of food becomes important. Easily digested carbohydrate food such as sugar, honey, and sweets cause a reaction like 'meal eating'. As can easily be seen, more slowly digested carbohydrates, as in whole grain cereals and vegetables, simulate 'nibbling'. Moreover rapidly absorbed carbohydrate evokes a rapid increase in blood sugar and hence in secretion of insulin. There is then a rapid fall to low levels of blood sugar and a return of hunger. More carbohydrate is then eaten and the process is repeated. Protein food and to a lesser extent slowly digested carbohydrate foods avoid this 'stop-go' response. We shall have more to say about carbohydrates when we come to deal with the importance of body water in overweight people.

The relationship of fluid retention to excessive weight is one which is obvious to the clinician, who can demonstrate in most fat women a pitting oedema over the shin bones. It is not clear why this should be less common in men. A possible explanation is the higher oestrogen levels in women. It is more likely to be found in the week before the menstrual period, when the oestrogen level is high, for oestrogens, as we have seen, encourage retention of fluid, but is detectable at other times. The cause is unknown; it is not due to hypothyroidism for it is often present in obese women with normal thyroid function. The sudden changes in weight often experienced by women may be unaccountable by changes in fat storage.

It is common for a woman's weight to increase by 4 or 5 pounds or more in the week before menstruation and to drop with a more or less obvious diuresis during the flow. This is easily explicable by cyclical changes in the ovarian secretions. But it is often possible to relate rapid changes in weight to emotional causes. This was discussed in chapter 12. Here it is enough to say that the brilliant researches of Verney suggest that an impulse passes from the frontal lobes of the brain via the hypothalamus and posterior pituitary to the tubules of the kidney and inhibit the production of urine. Von Grafe wrote: 'fatty tissues absorb water like a sponge without circulatory disturbances and with no evidence of oedema,' but in fact oedema is often demonstrable.

It used to be assumed that anxiety causes loss of weight and it is indeed true that some people when worried lose their appetites. Others as we have seen raid the larder. But changes in the water content of the tissues may cut across these deviations from the normal. For instance, an intelligent and well-educated married woman of 28, 5 ft 2 in in height, weighed 8 st 7 lb until August 1941, when she learned that her husband was missing. She was desperately depressed by the news, sometimes prostrate with grief at the thought of his possible death, at others tortured by the thought of his possible maltreatment by his captors. She began immediately to gain weight. In May 1942 she weighed 11 stones. She had complete amenorrhoea during this period and suffered from breathlessness on exertion and palpitations of the heart. On examination in May 1942, she was found to be very obese, with obvious oedema of the ankles and shins. Nothing else abnormal was found and a complete investigation failed to find any cardiac or renal cause of the oedema. Treatment in hospital with a diet poor in carbohydrates and with urea reduced her weight to 9 st 13 lb, but when she returned to her occupation as a physical training instructress she rapidly regained her previous weight. She volunteered the information that she always lost weight if she rested a lot: the diuretic effect of recumbency is well known. During 1943 she emerged from her despondency and formed an attachment for a wealthy man who took her daily to the best restaurants. She ceased to follow her diet. Her weight fell rapidly to about 9 stones and menstruation returned to normal. A second woman of 29, 5 ft 3 in in height, was fairly slim until June 1945, when she weighed 10 st 4 lb. Her only child then developed otitis media and afterwards mastoiditis. The mother, who was extremely anxious, began to get fatter. The mastoiditis was followed by a series of complications. She was first seen in March 1946, when her weight was

12 st 10 lb. The child was still in hospital and the mother so distressed that she was unable to talk of the illness without tears. Nothing abnormal could be found other than corpulence and pitting oedema of the ankles and shins. She lost weight when her child recovered. A third woman observed during the war habitually increased in weight when her husband was away and lost it with a dramatic diuresis whenever he returned.

The degree of fluid retention complicating true adiposity is affected profoundly by diet. It need hardly be stressed that eating large quantities of salt is bound to be followed by the retention of enough water to keep the tissue fluid at normal concentration. Carbohydrate is once more the criminal. A high carbohydrate diet given to an obese patient may cause a retention of a litre a day of water and naturally of enough salt. If obese people are maintained on water only they lose salt, but if carbohydrate is added to their diet they cease to do so. If equal quantities of protein or fat are added their loss of salt (and therefore of fluid) is increased. The water retaining capacity of carbohydrate is actually greater than that of salt. It has been calculated that 0·9 gm of salt have a water-retaining potential of 100 ml, whereas the same weight of glucose would cause the retention of 500 ml. A fairly mild indulgence in $\frac{1}{4}$ lb of sweets (say 100 gm of glucose) would thus be capable of increasing the weight rapidly by about 100 lb. Happily the hypothalamus and the kidneys can usually deal effectively with the load.

Much of this chapter may be read as an attack on a high carbohydrate intake in the diet, and it may be useful to summarise the points made.

1 Carbohydrate foods like sugar, cereals and potatoes are especially suitable for the lazy housewife and lazy eater. Few

need cooking and none need chewing. They are also cheap. They therefore are often eaten excessively.

2 Carbohydrate is the precursor of fat.

3 Carbohydrate, especially sugar, has a low 'satiety value': it relieves hunger rapidly but only for a short time.

4 Carbohydrate prevents the formation of a fat mobilising factor, whereas fat encourages it.

5 Carbohydrate, especially sugar, is rapidly absorbed, a fact that encourages its change to fat in the adipose tissue.

6 Carbohydrate causes fluid retention.

It is difficult to overestimate the importance of avoiding corpulence. Nevertheless an obsession about weight has its dangers, some already described in chapter 12. It is better to be too thin than too fat, but *in media via tutissimus ibis*.

Epilogue

Endocrinology is advancing so fast that this book is already out of date as it lies in your hands. Happily most of the advances in the next year will probably be highly technical and unsuited to a book that is intended for the scientifically-minded layman and student and not for the medical practitioner. There will be new and better methods of determining the amount of each hormone in blood and urine. Methods such as chromatography and electrophoresis in the study of endocrinology, new though they are, are already in the process of being supplanted for some purposes by immunological and radiological techniques. Radioassay has made it possible to determine the amount of thyroxine, cortisol, progesterone, oestradiol and testosterone in blood in a few hours. As little as a millionth of a milligram of progesterone can, it is claimed, be measured in one millilitre of plasma or the cortisol in one hundredth of a millilitre. If these claims stand up to criticism, the diagnosis and elucidation of endocrine disorders will be made far easier. Already the clinical endocrinologist, burdened as he must be by the status of the perpetual student, is compensated by the dramatic results of his treatment of the afflicted, though sometimes saddened by the failure of many doctors to diagnose and treat so many distressing but tractable disorders. New methods of blood analysis must inevitably broaden his scope.

Nevertheless, endocrinology will remain a part of general medicine and we may be confident that the new techniques of biochemistry will have their repercussions not only on the disorders of the ductless glands themselves but on the management of the disorders of every part of the body.

Recommended further reading

General endocrinology

R. H. Williams (ed.), *Textbook of Endocrinology* (4th edn), Saunders (London and Philadelphia), 1968.

G. Jasmin (ed.), *Endocrine Aspects of Disease Processes*, Heinemann (London), 1969.

P. C. Clegg, *Introduction to Mechanisms of Hormone Action*, Heinemann (London), 1969.

The pituitary gland

G. W. Harris and B. T. Donovan, *The Pituitary Gland*, Butterworth (London), University of California Press (Berkeley), 1966.

The adrenal gland

C. L. Cope, *Adrenal Steroids and Disease*, Pitman (London), Lippincott (Philadelphia), 1965.

The thyroid gland

J. H. Means, L. J. de Groot and J. B. Stanbury, *The Thyroid and Its Diseases* (3rd edn), McGraw-Hill (London and New York), 1963.

R. Pitt-Rivers and J. R. Tata, *The Thyroid Hormones*, Pergamon (Oxford and New York), 1959.

The ovaries

P. M. F. Bishop, *Gynaecological Endocrinology* (3rd edn), Livingstone (Edinburgh and New York), 1970.

D. G. Ferriman, *Anovulatory Infertility*, Heinemann (London), 1969.

S. Zuckerman (*et al.*), *The Ovary*, Academic Press (London and New York), 1962.

The testicles

G. E. W. Wolstenholme and M. O'Connor, *Endocrinology of the Testis*, Churchill (London), Little, Brown and Co. (Boston), 1967.

The thyroid-parathyroid partnership

S. Taylor, *Calcitonin* (2 vols.), Heinemann (London), 1968 and 1970.

The pancreas
W.G.Oakley, D.A.Pyke and K.W.Taylor, *Clinical Diabetes and its Biochemical Basis*, Blackwell (Oxford and New York), 1968.
V.Marks and F.C.Rose, *Hypoglycaemia*, Blackwell (Oxford), Davis (Philadelphia), 1965.

Hormones and behaviour
R.P.Michael (ed.), *Endocrinology and Human Behaviour*, Oxford University Press (Oxford and New York), 1968.
K.Dalton, *The Premenstrual Syndrome*, Heinemann (London), Thomas (New York), 1964.

Hormones and digestion
R.A.Gregory, *Secretory Mechanisms of the Gastro-intestinal Tract*, Monograph of the Physiological Society No. 11, Arnold (London), Williams and Wilkins (Baltimore), 1962.

Hormones and the cardiovascular system
W.L.Ashton, *Human Atheroma*, Heinemann (London), 1967.

Hormones and muscle
R.Greene, *Myasthenia Gravis*, Heinemann (London), 1969.

Acknowledgments

Acknowledgment is due to the following for the illustrations (the number refers to the page on which the illustration appears): 64–5 Dr F.C.Kelly, the Chilean Iodine Education Bureau; 88 adapted from S.Soskin and R.Levine, *Carbohydrate Metabolism*, University of Chicago Press, 1946; 195 the Dean and Chapter of Westminster Abbey; 214 the Director of the National Portrait Gallery, London.

The diagrams were drawn by Design Practitioners Limited.